Real World Colouring Book

For Advanced Users & Adults

50 Images

Created From Real Life Photos For You To Colour As You Please.

ISBN 978-0-359-82283-6
90000
9 780359 822836

GH POST OFFICE
ONE WAY
SQUARE

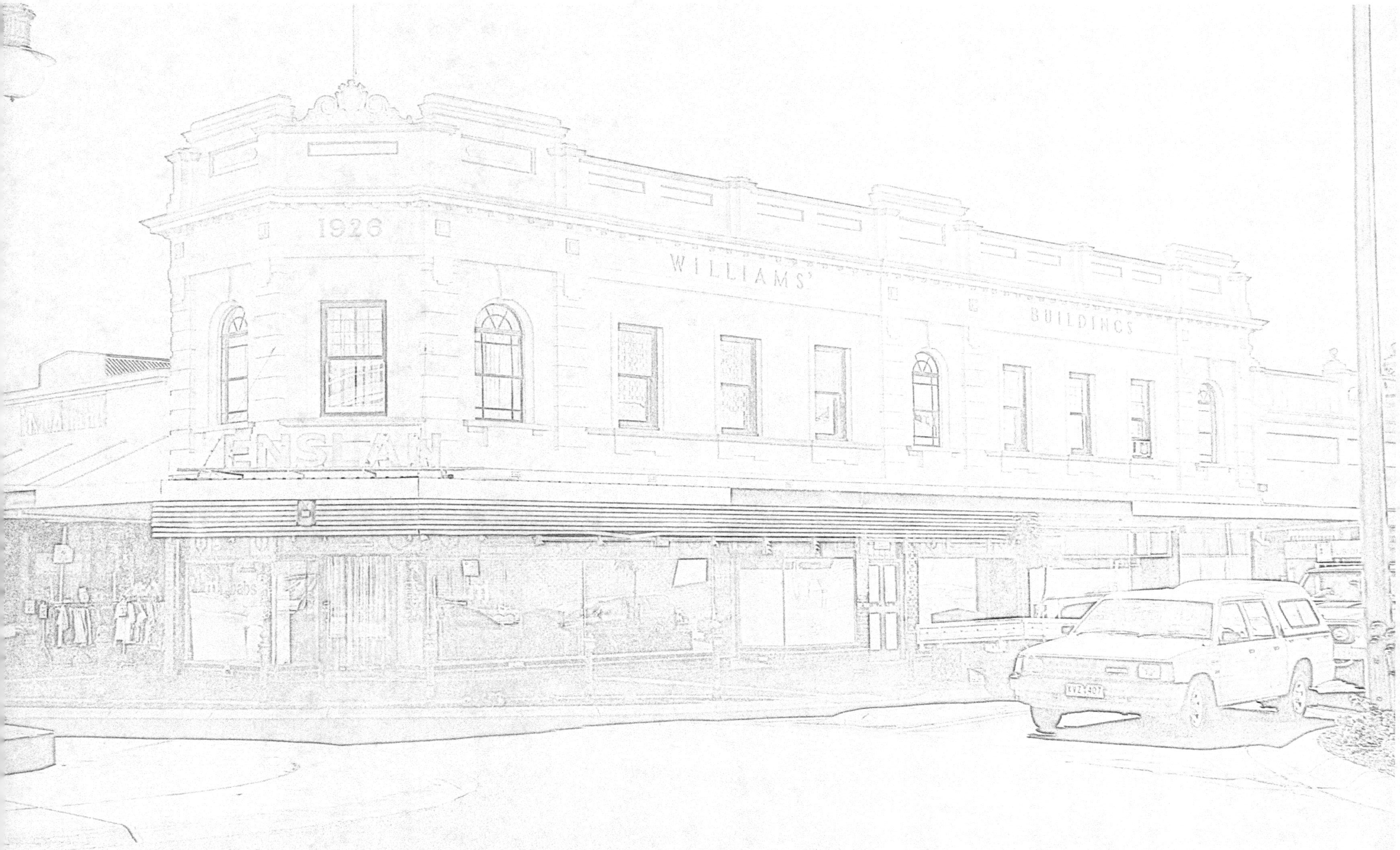
1926
WILLIAMS' BUILDINGS

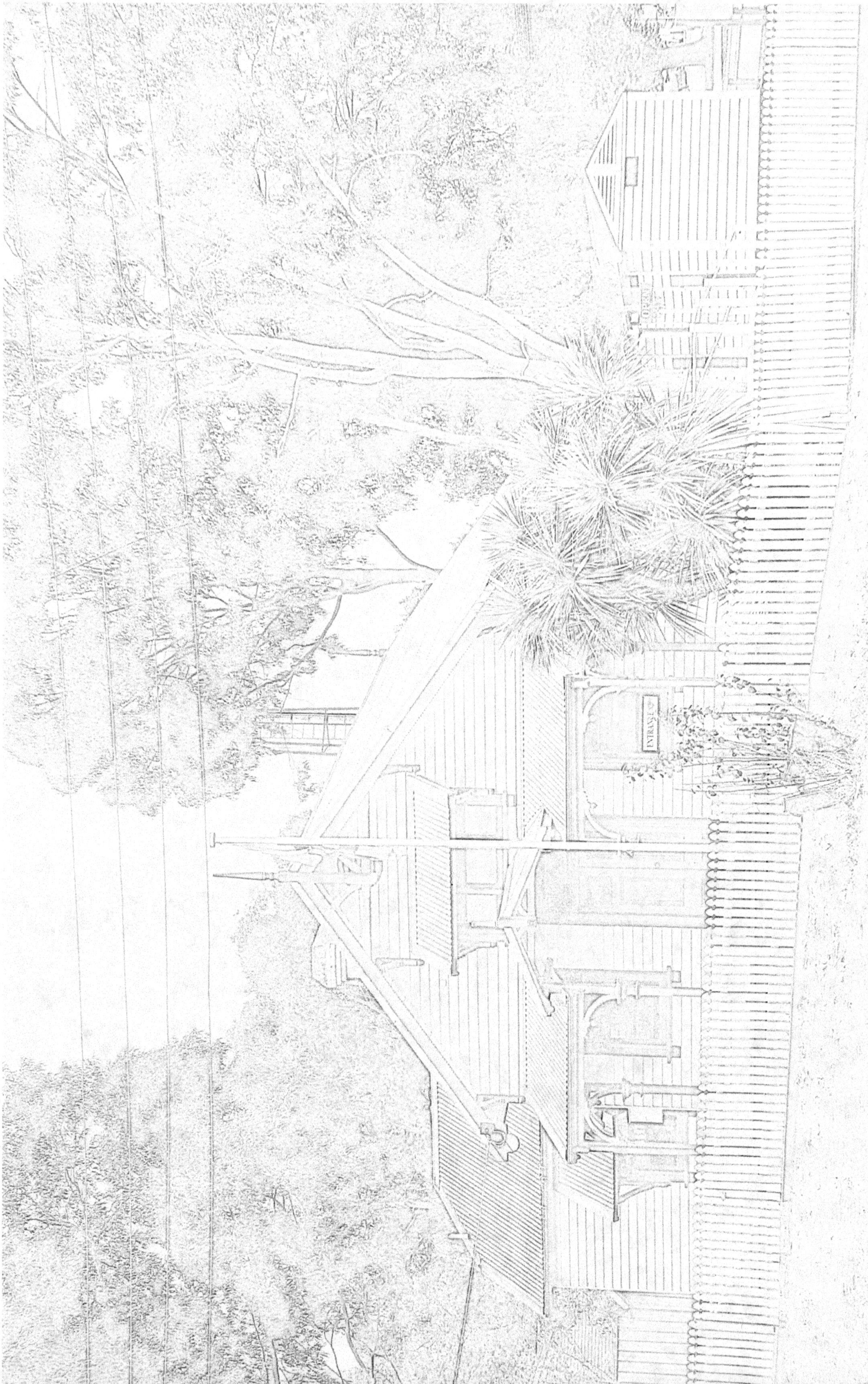
ENTRANCE

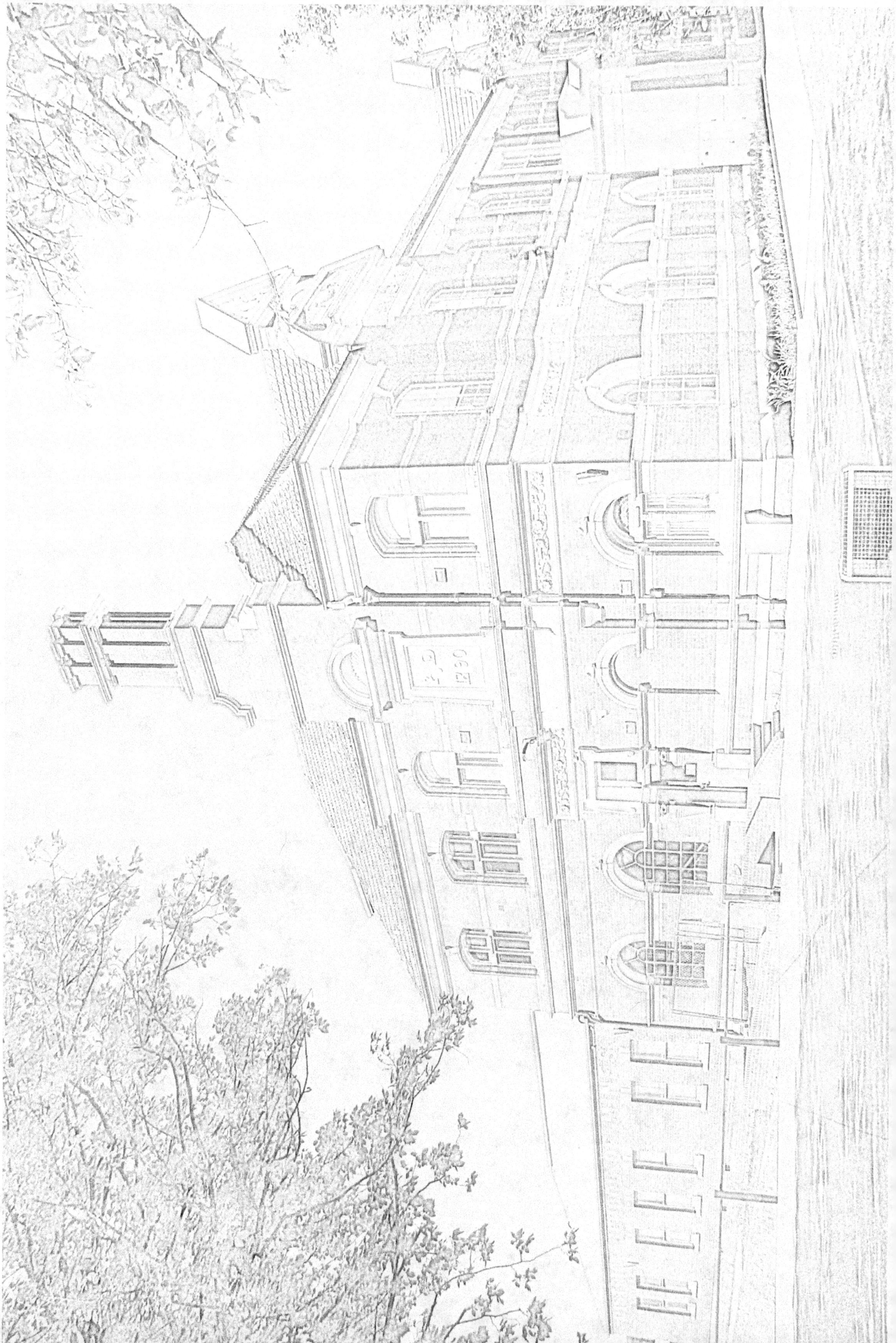

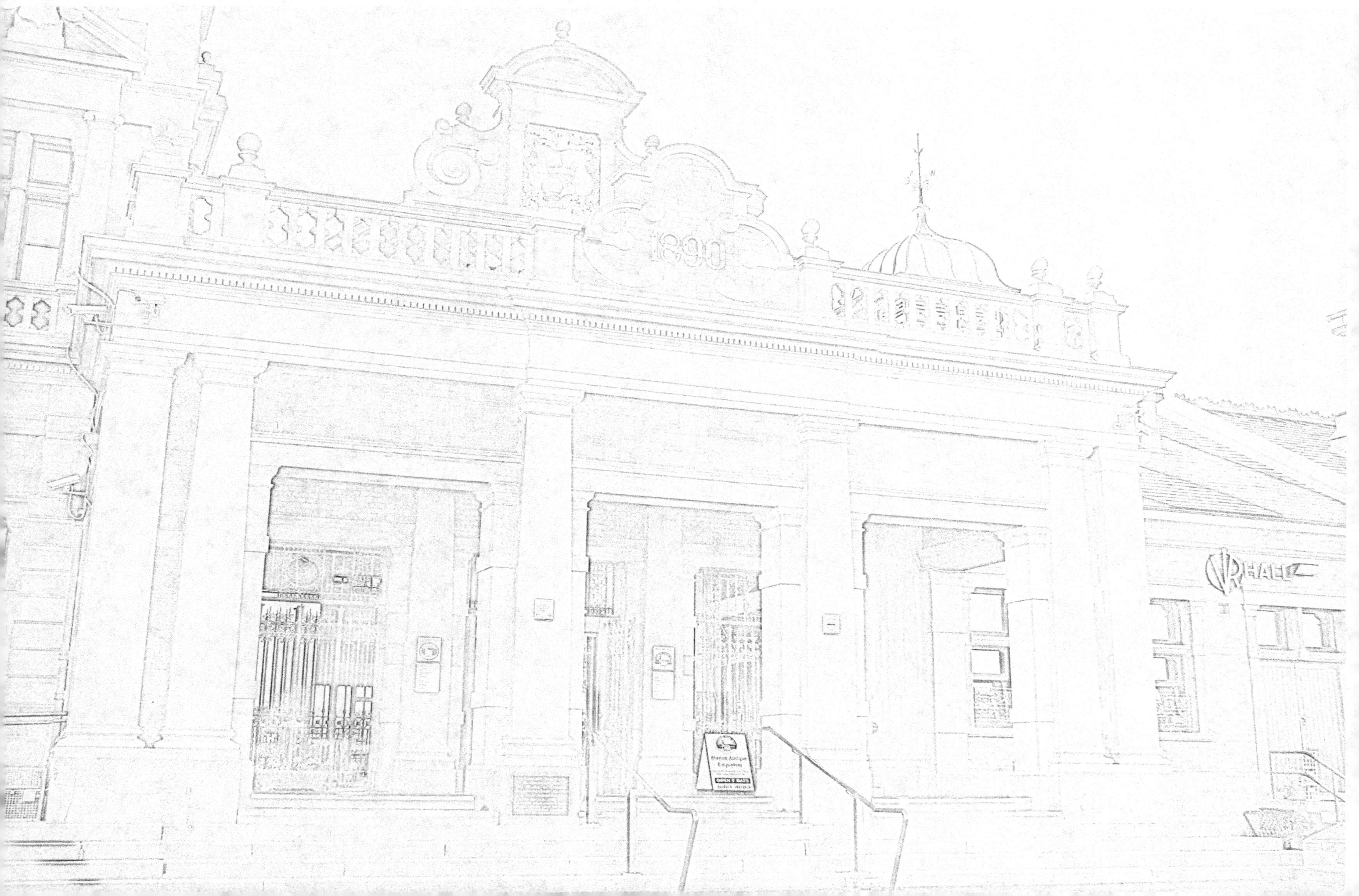

1890
Station Antique
Emporium
HALL

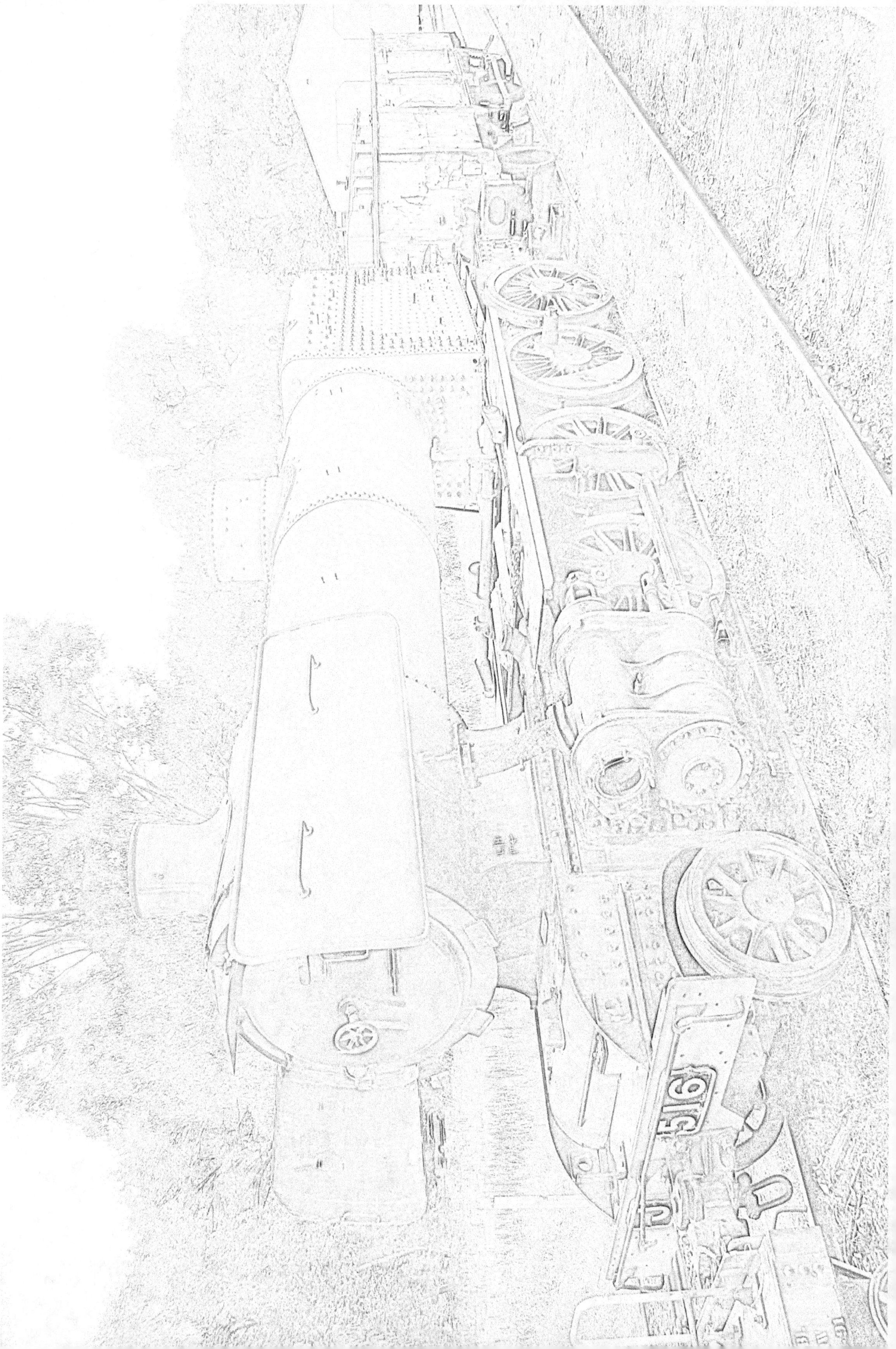

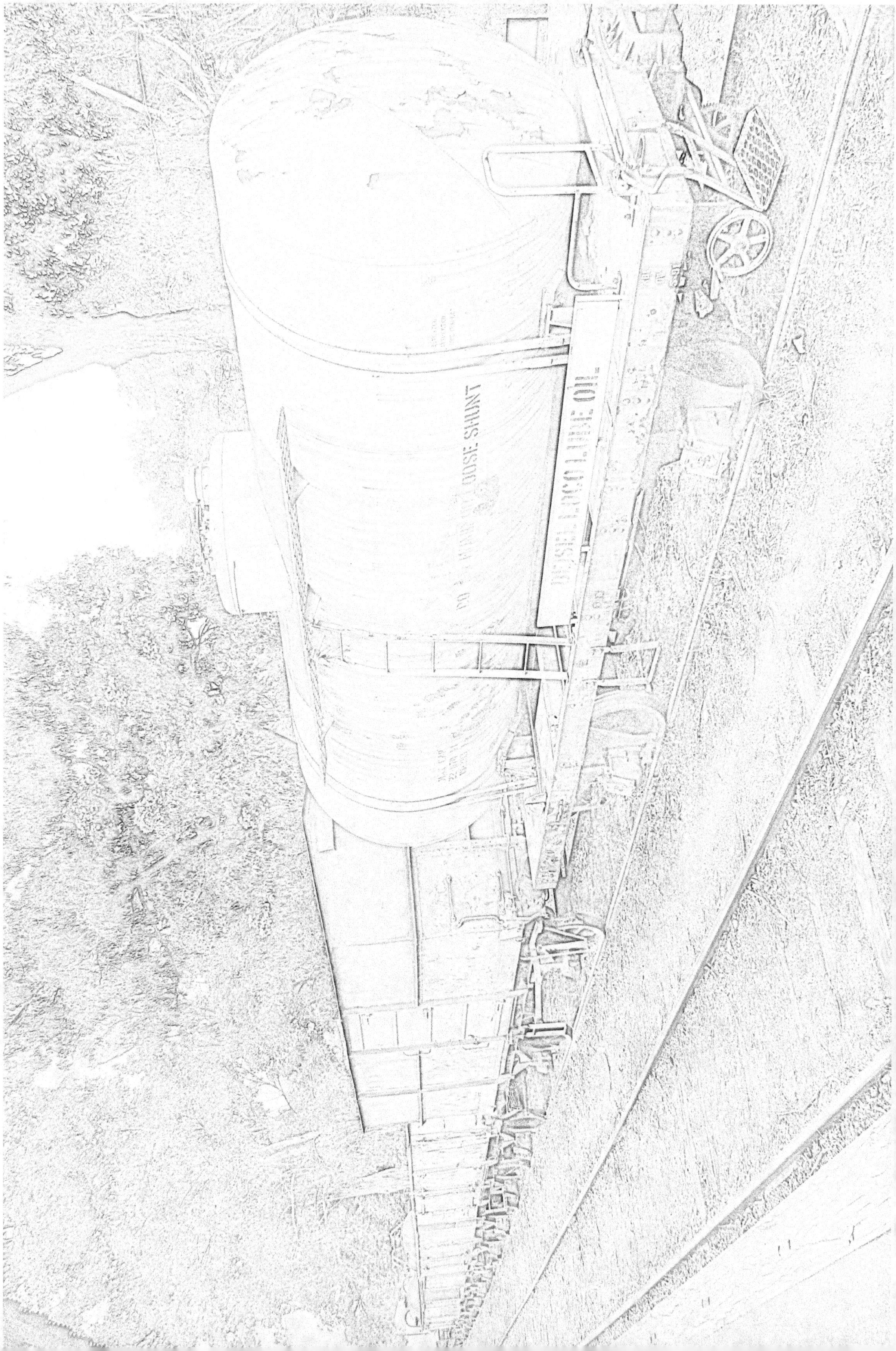
DIESEL LOCO. LUBE OIL

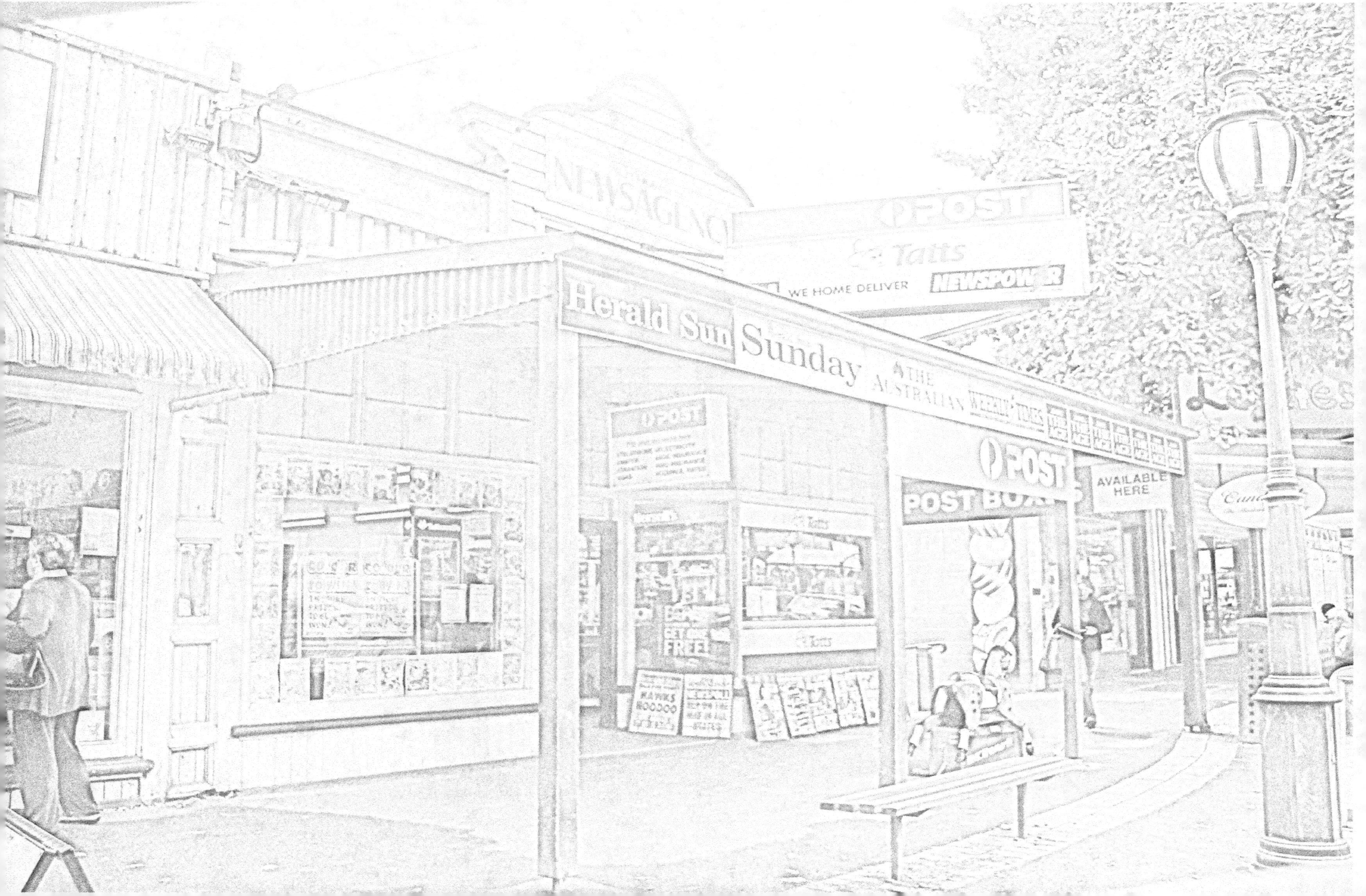
POST
Tatts
WE HOME DELIVER
NEWSPOWER
Herald Sun
Sunday
THE AUSTRALIAN
POST
POST BOX
AVAILABLE HERE
GET ONE FREE
HAWKS HOODOO

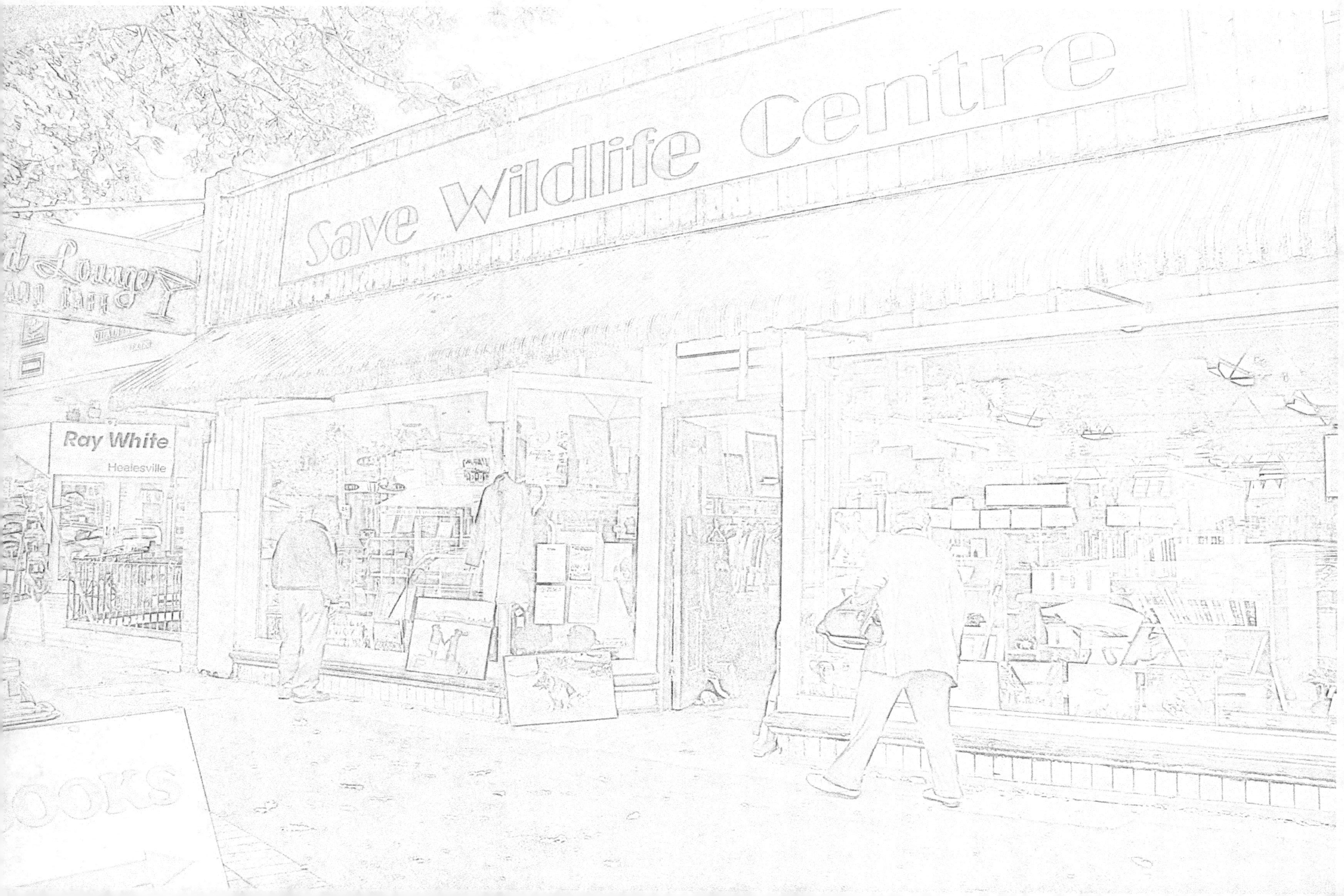
Save Wildlife Centre
Ray White
Healesville

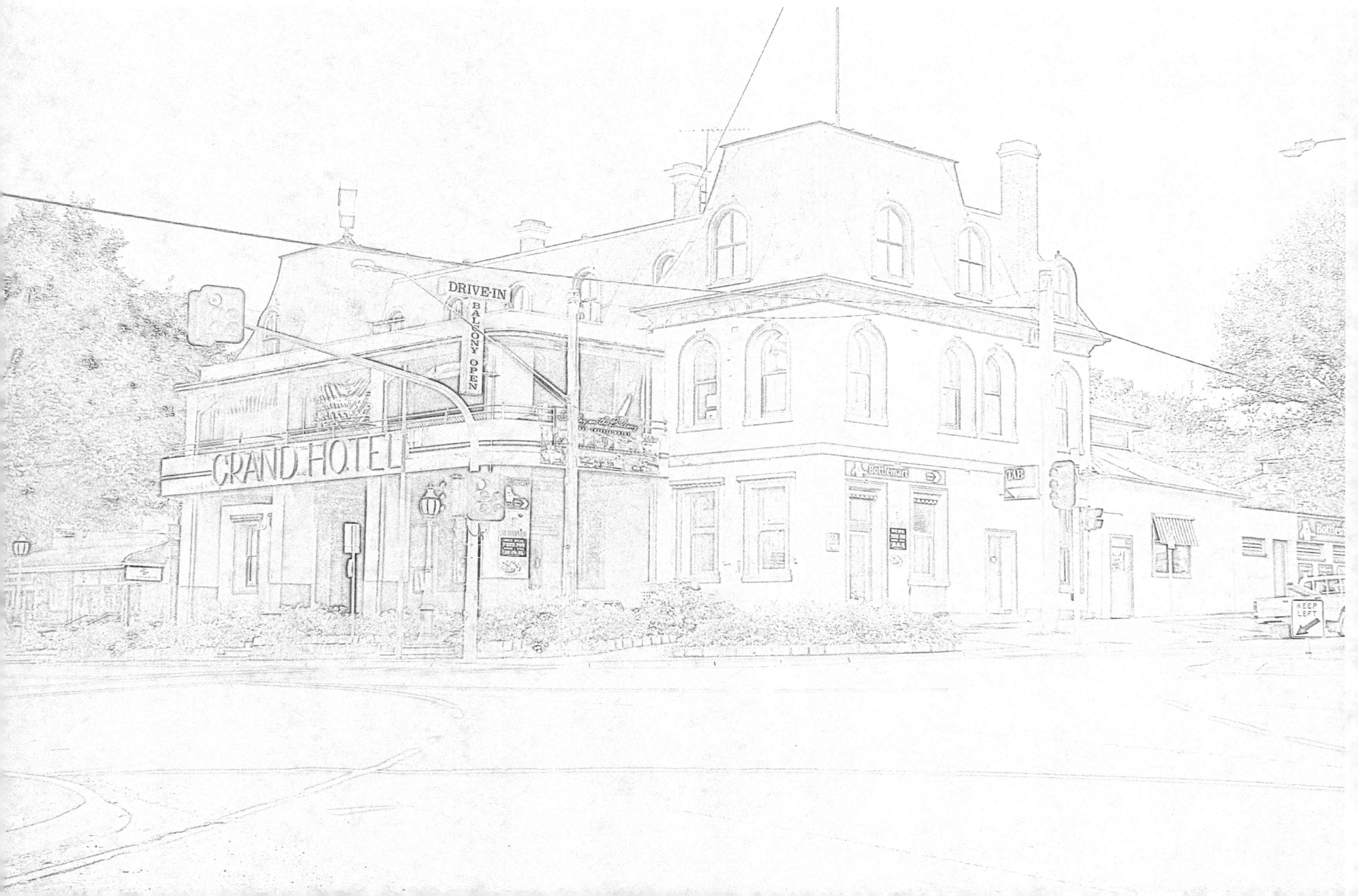
DRIVE-IN
BALCONY OPEN
GRAND HOTEL
Bottlemart
TAB
KEEP LEFT

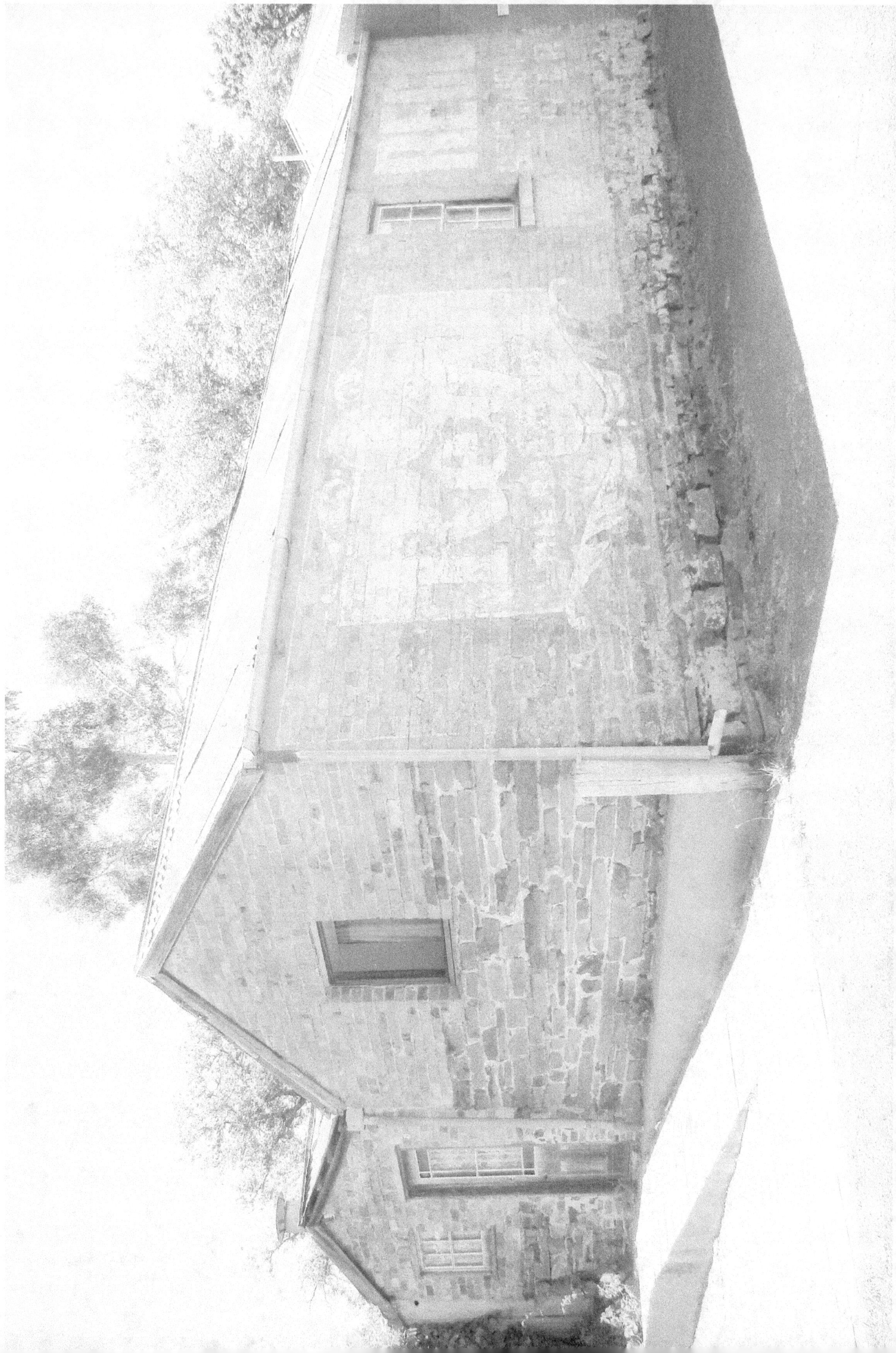

BEEHIVE
OLD WARES
& COLLECTABLES
FURNITURE
OLD WARES
COLLECTABLES
OPEN

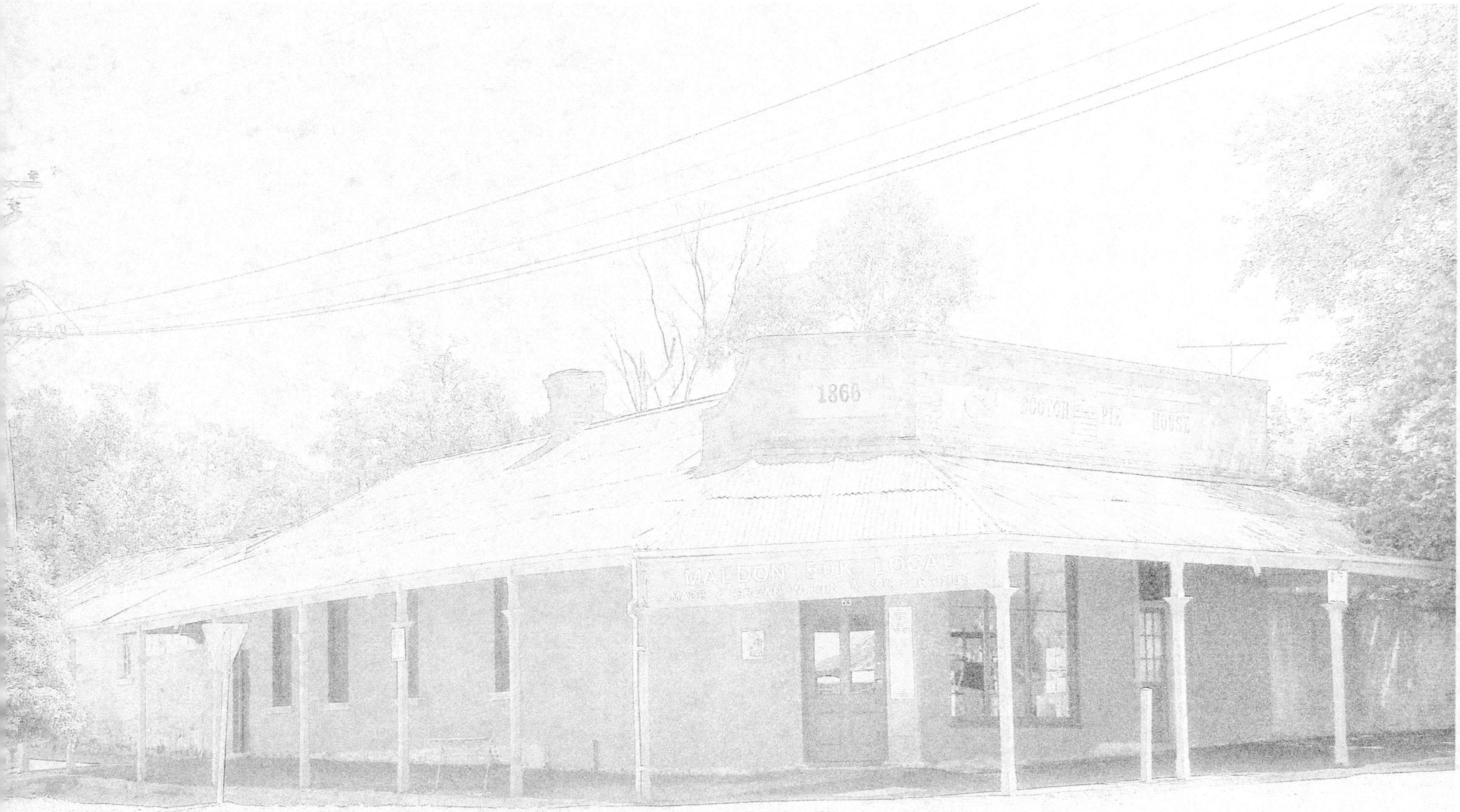
1866
SCOTCH PIE HOUSE
MALDON 50K LOCAL
MADE & GROWN
63

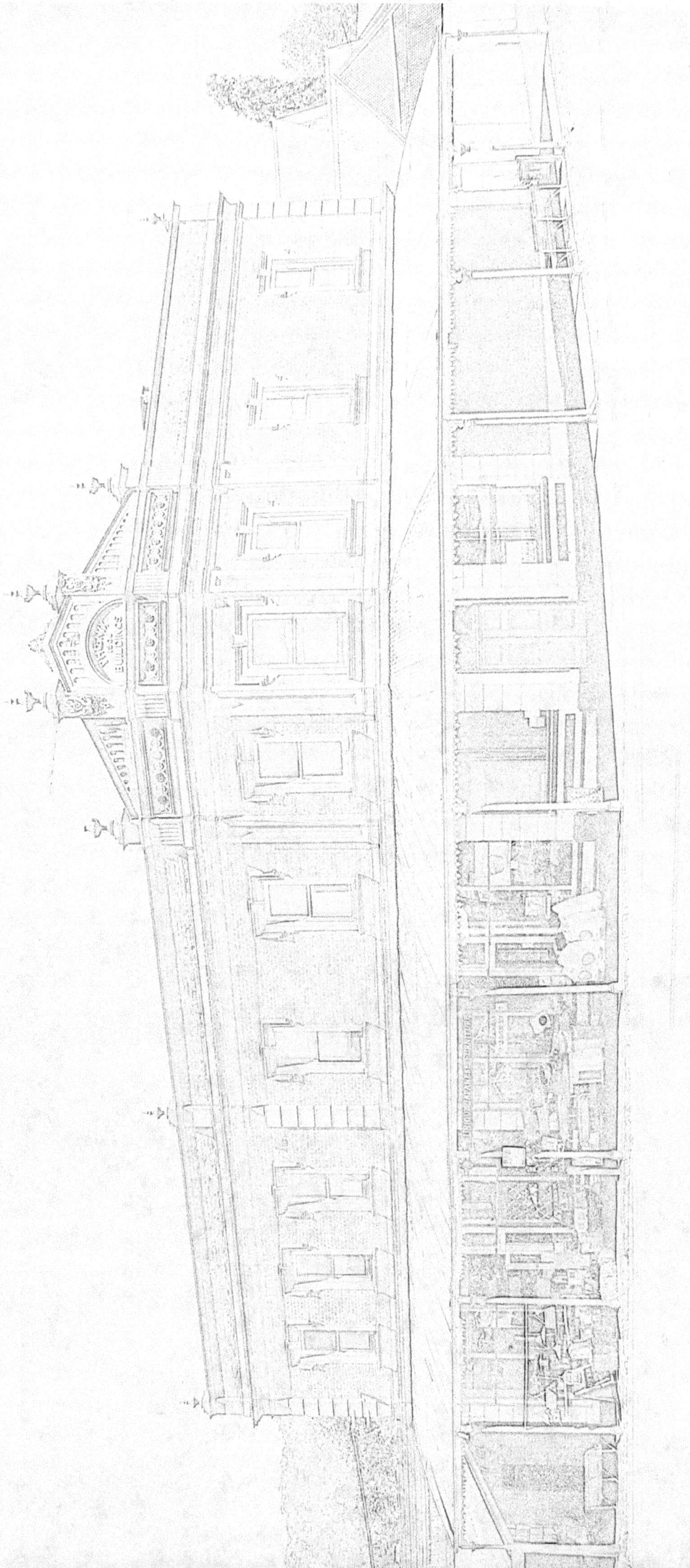

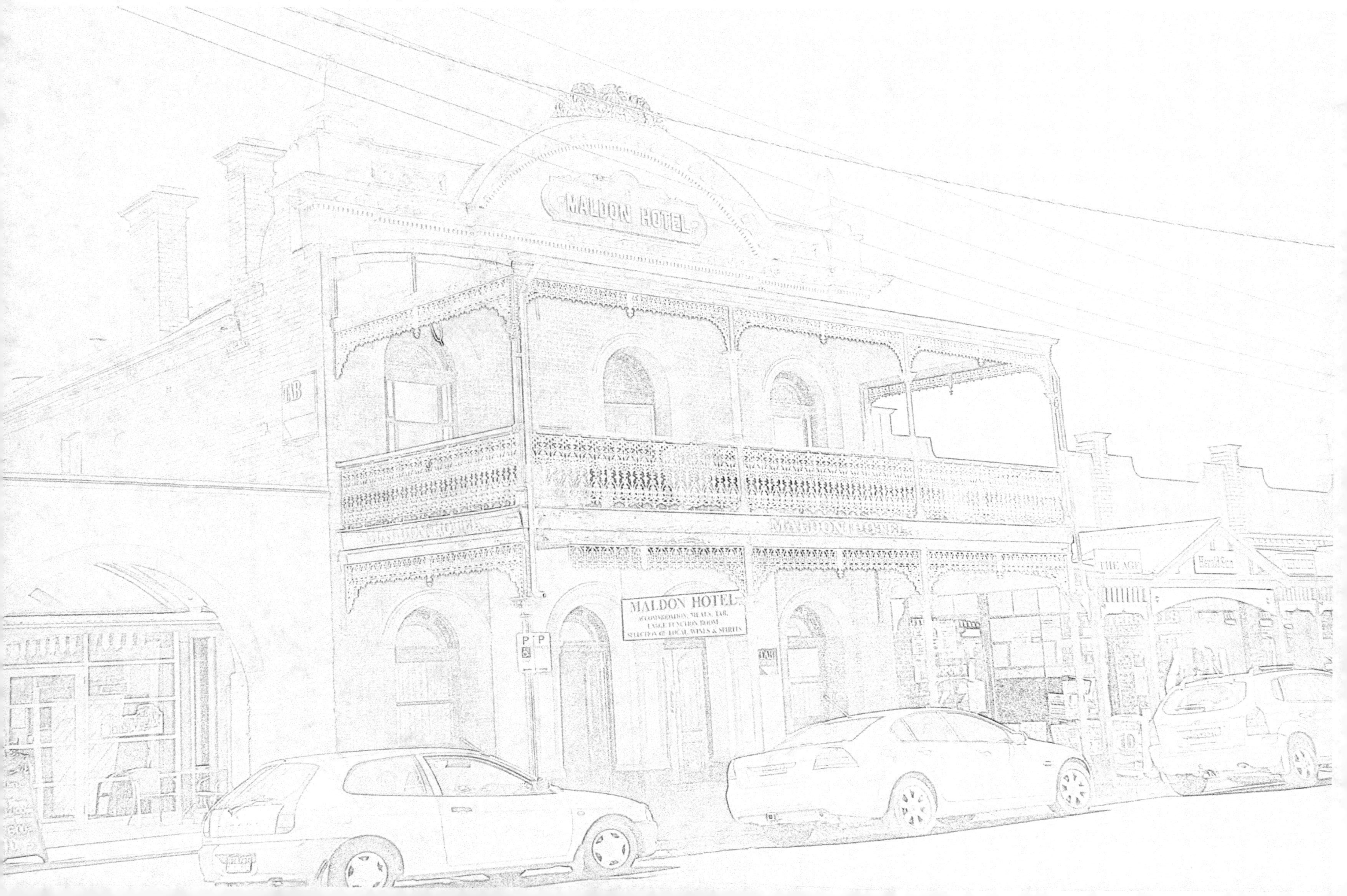
MALDON HOTEL
MALDON HOTEL
MALDON HOTEL
ACCOMMODATION, MEALS, TAB,
LARGE FUNCTION ROOM
SELECTION OF LOCAL WINES & SPIRITS
TAB
THE AGE
HeraldSun

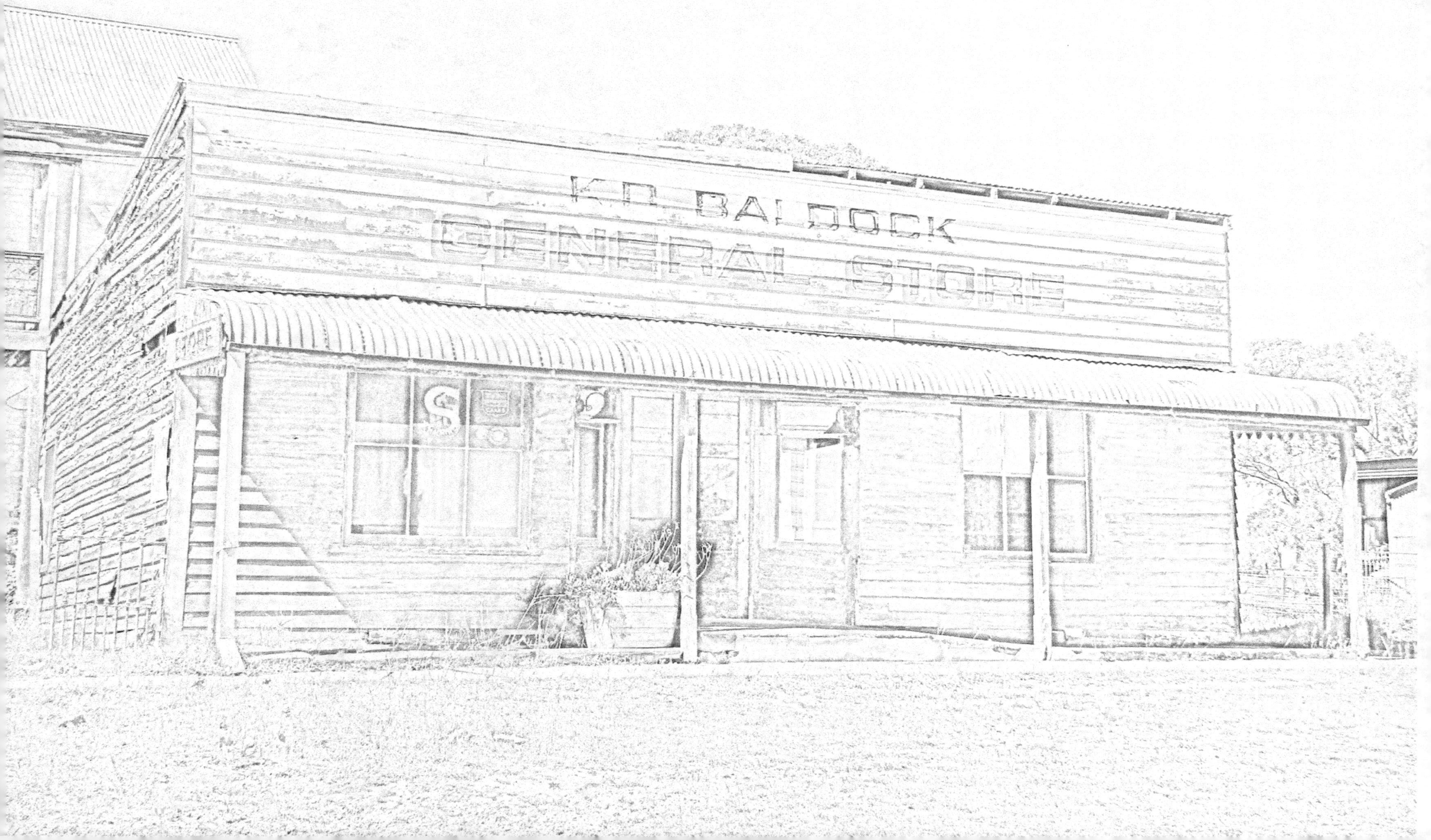
BALDOCK
GENERAL STORE

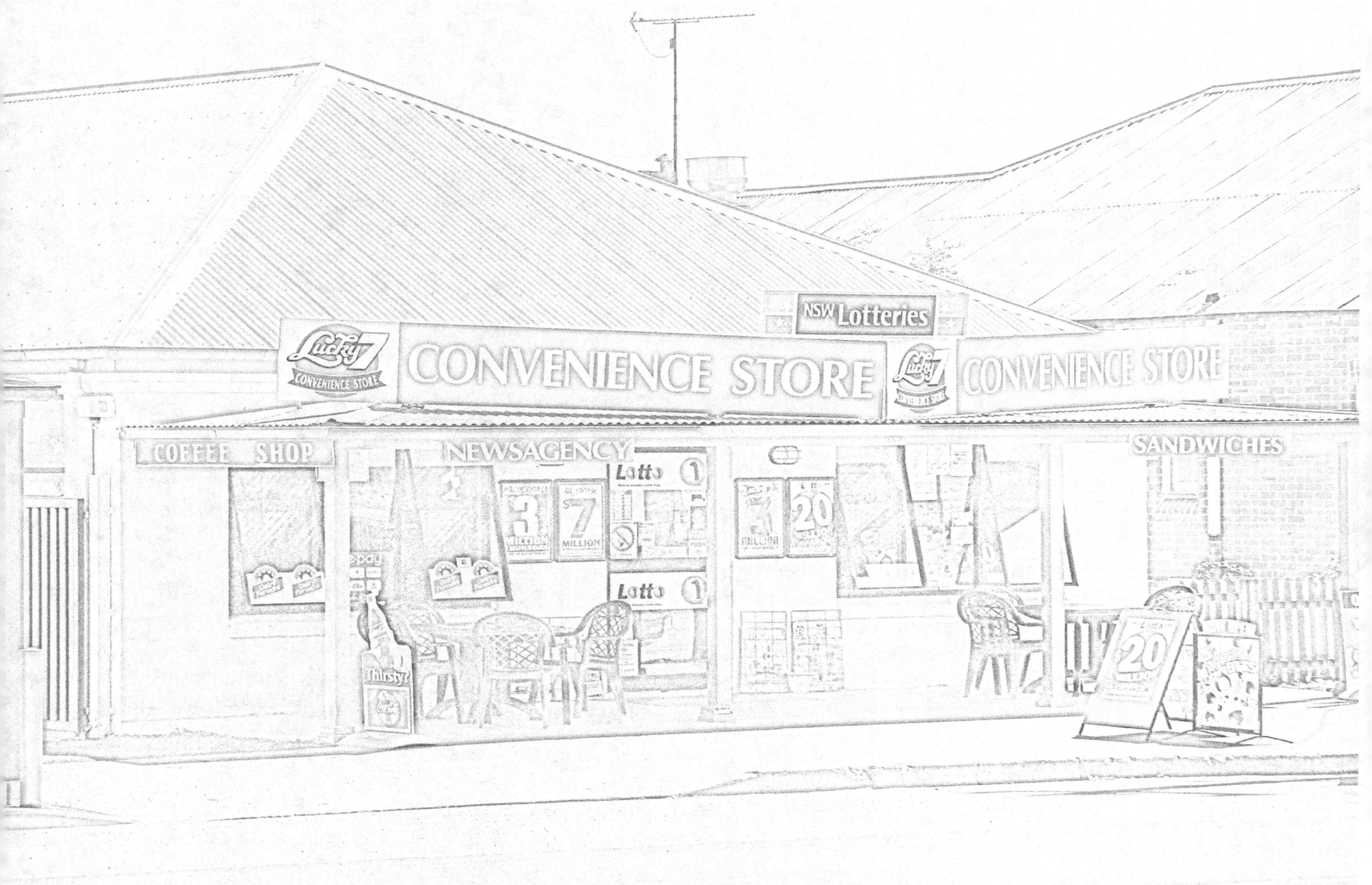
NSW Lotteries
Lucky 7
CONVENIENCE STORE
CONVENIENCE STORE
Lucky 7
CONVENIENCE STORE
CONVENIENCE STORE
COFFEE SHOP
NEWSAGENCY
SANDWICHES
Lotto
1
3
MILLION
$7
MILLION
Lotto
1
3
MILLION
20
Thirsty?
20

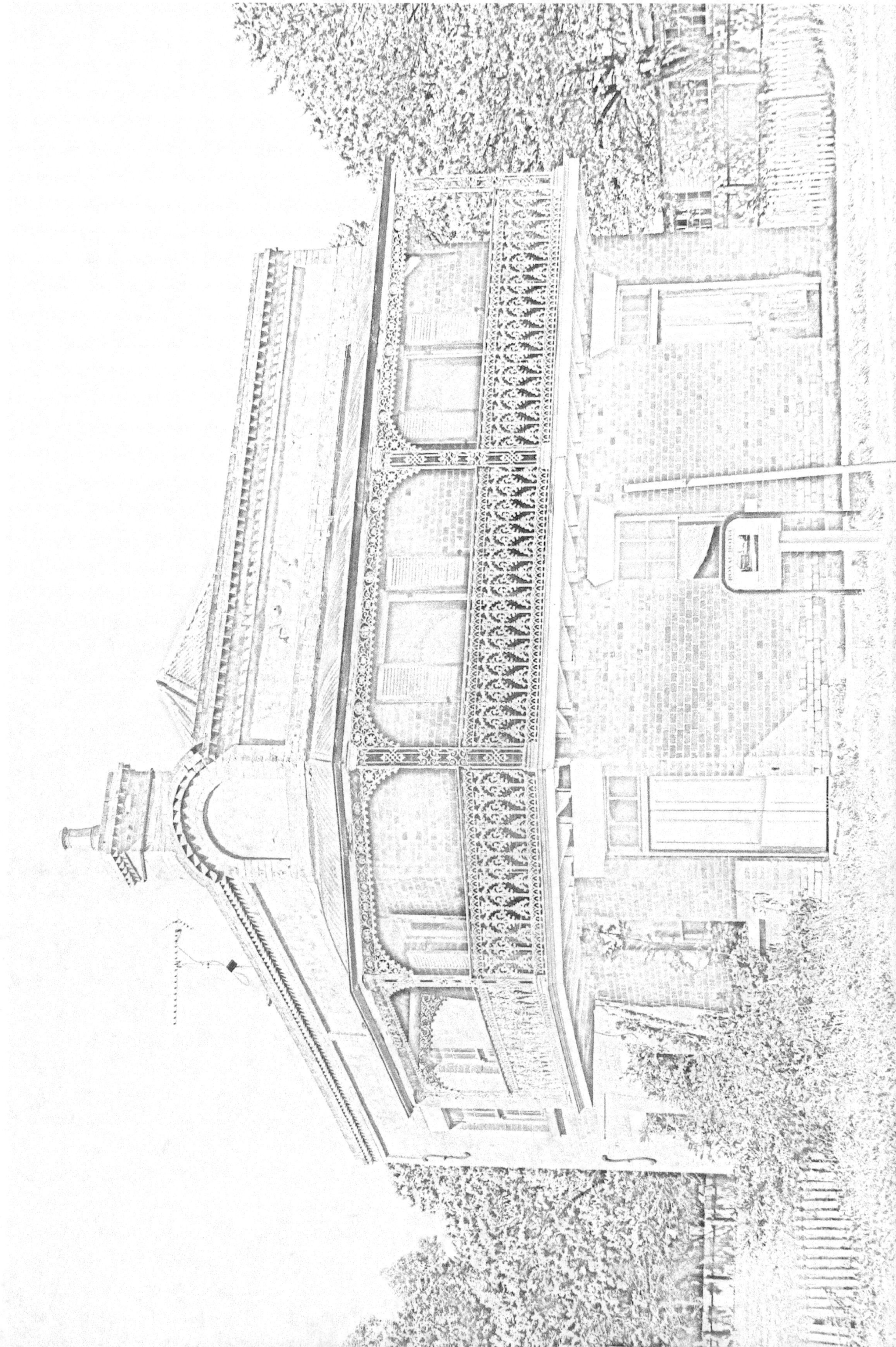

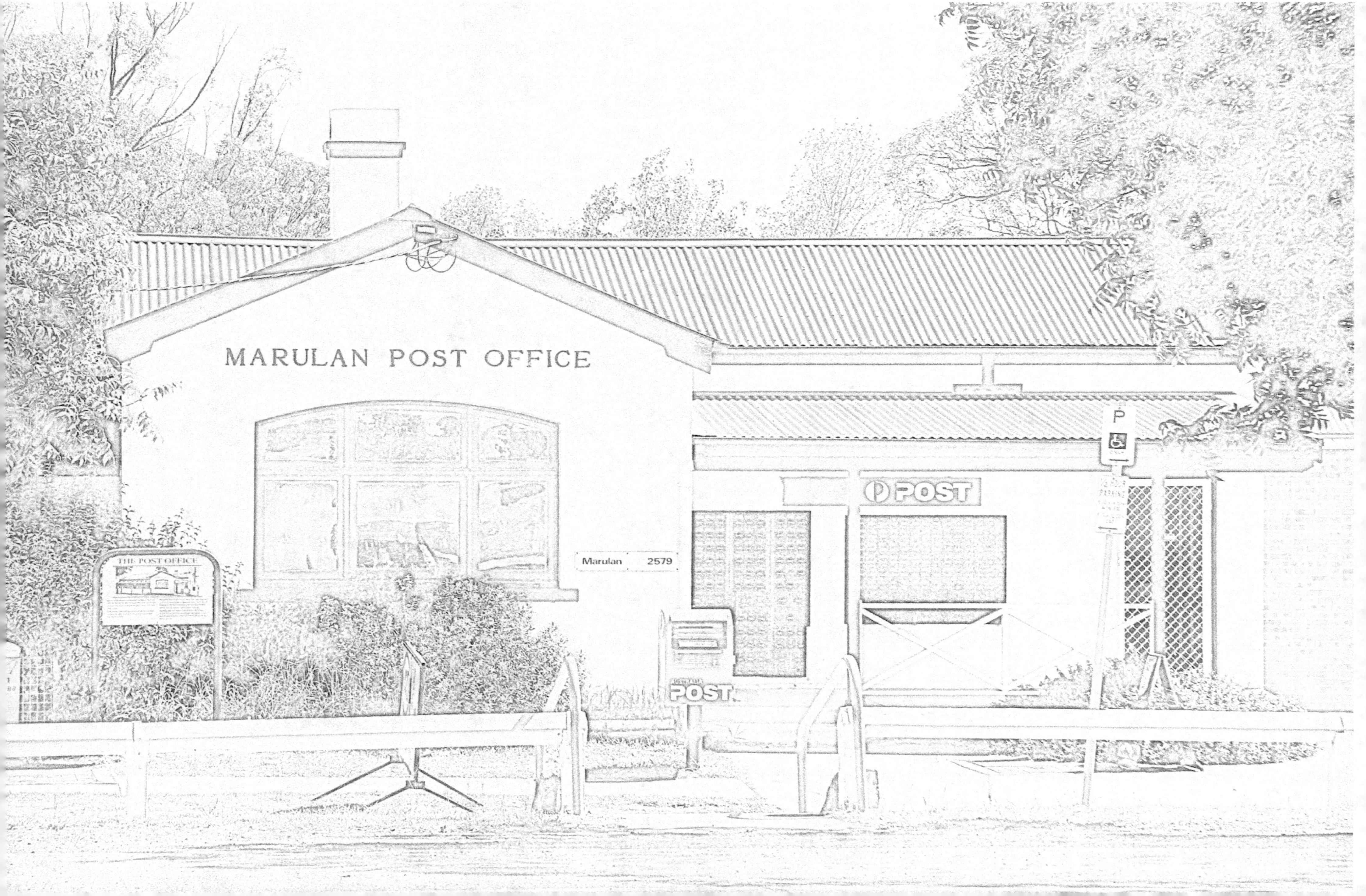
MARULAN POST OFFICE
THE POST OFFICE
Marulan 2579
POST
POST
P

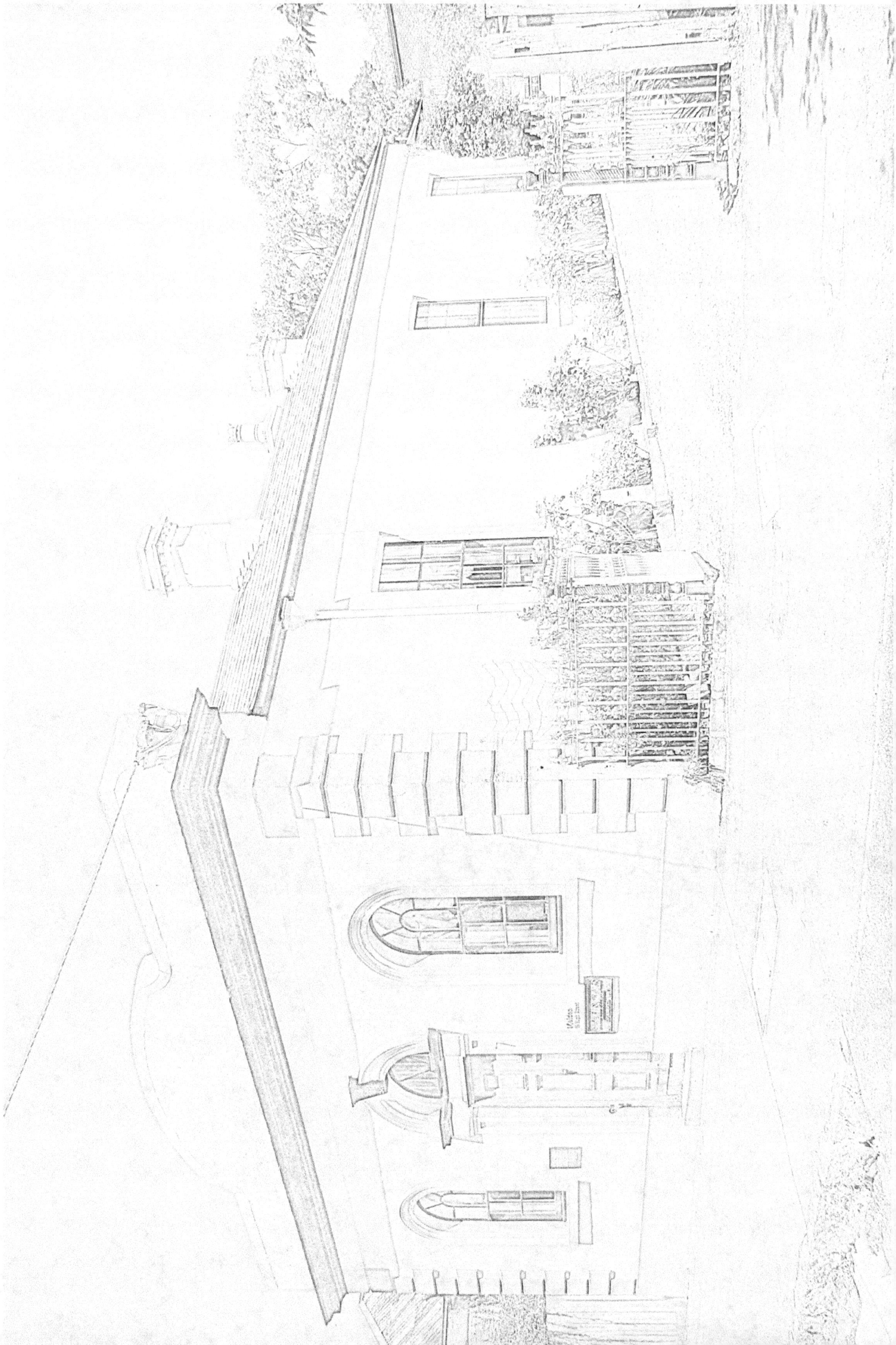

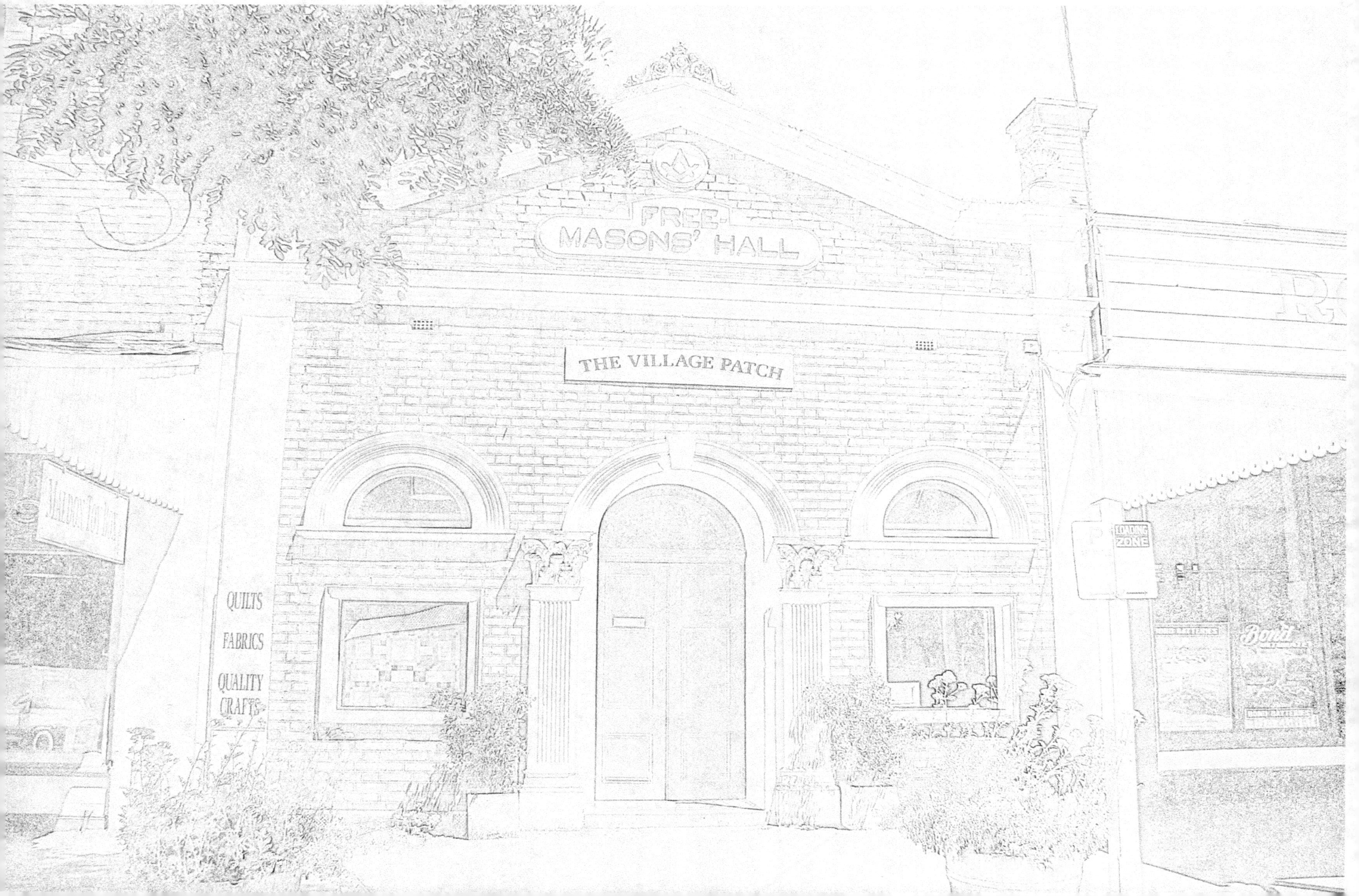
FREE-
MASONS' HALL
THE VILLAGE PATCH
QUILTS
FABRICS
QUALITY
CRAFTS
LOADING
ZONE

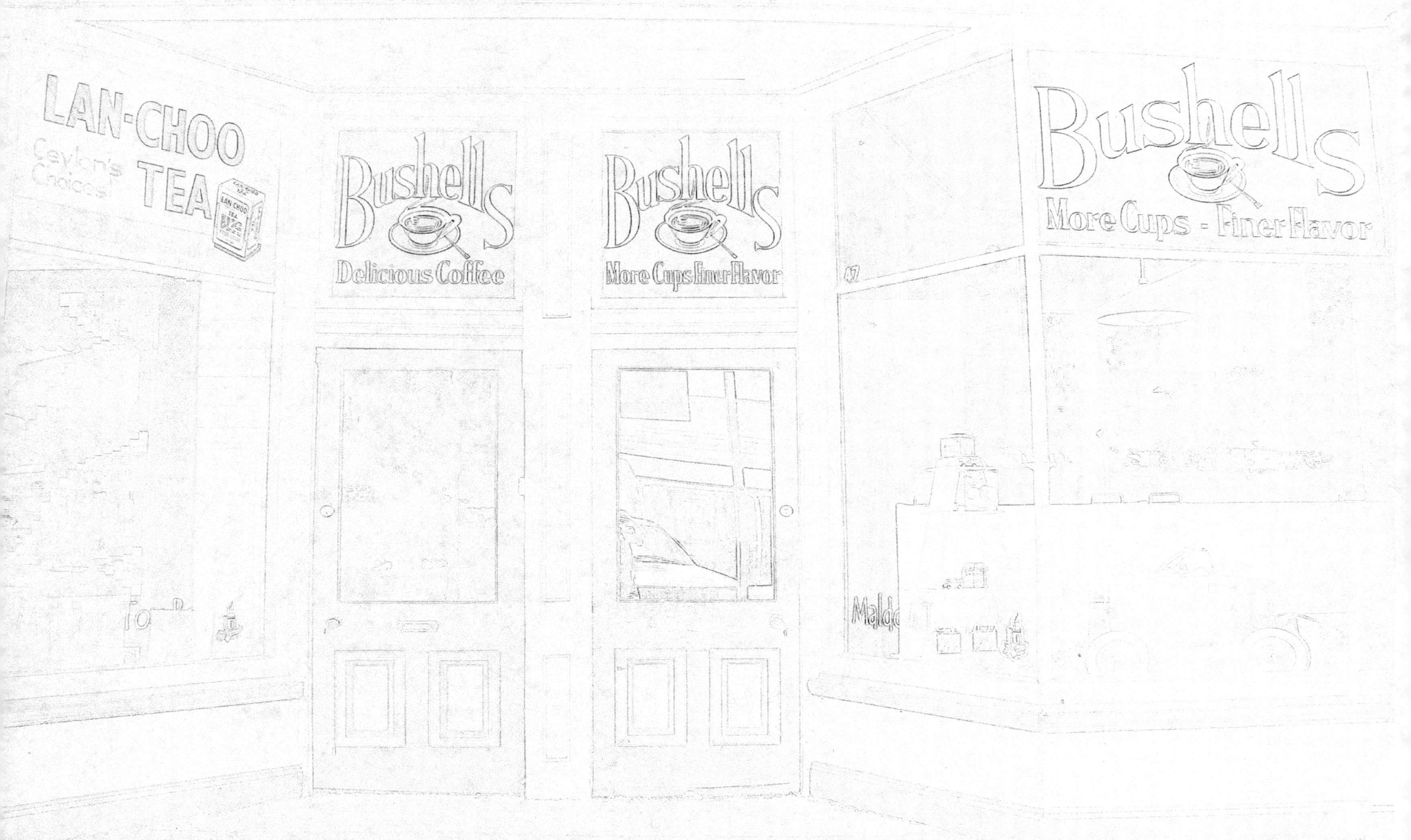

LAN-CHOO
Ceylon's Choicest
TEA
Bushells
Delicious Coffee
Bushells
More Cups Finer Flavor
Bushells
More Cups - Finer Flavor

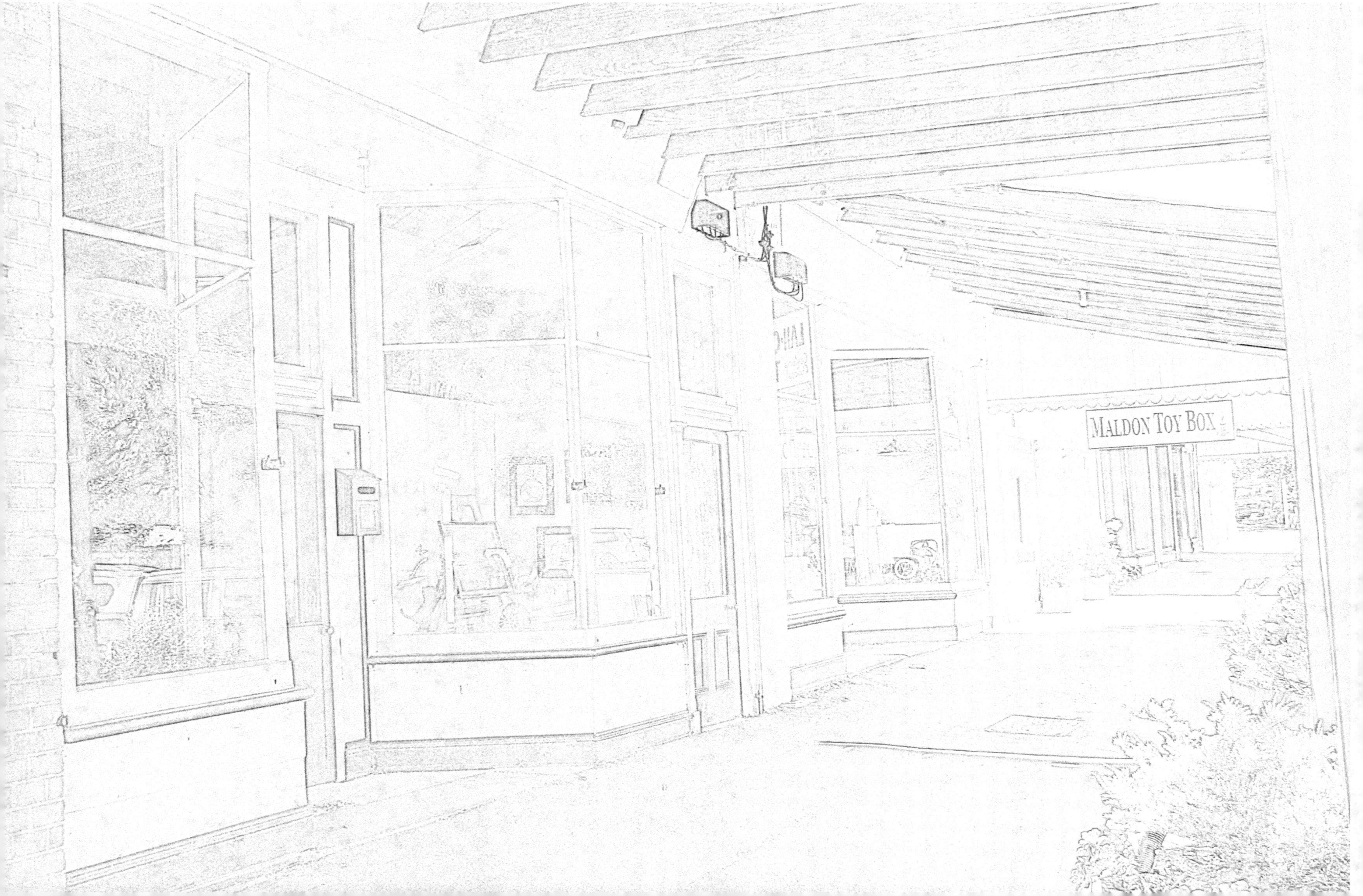
MALDON TOY BOX

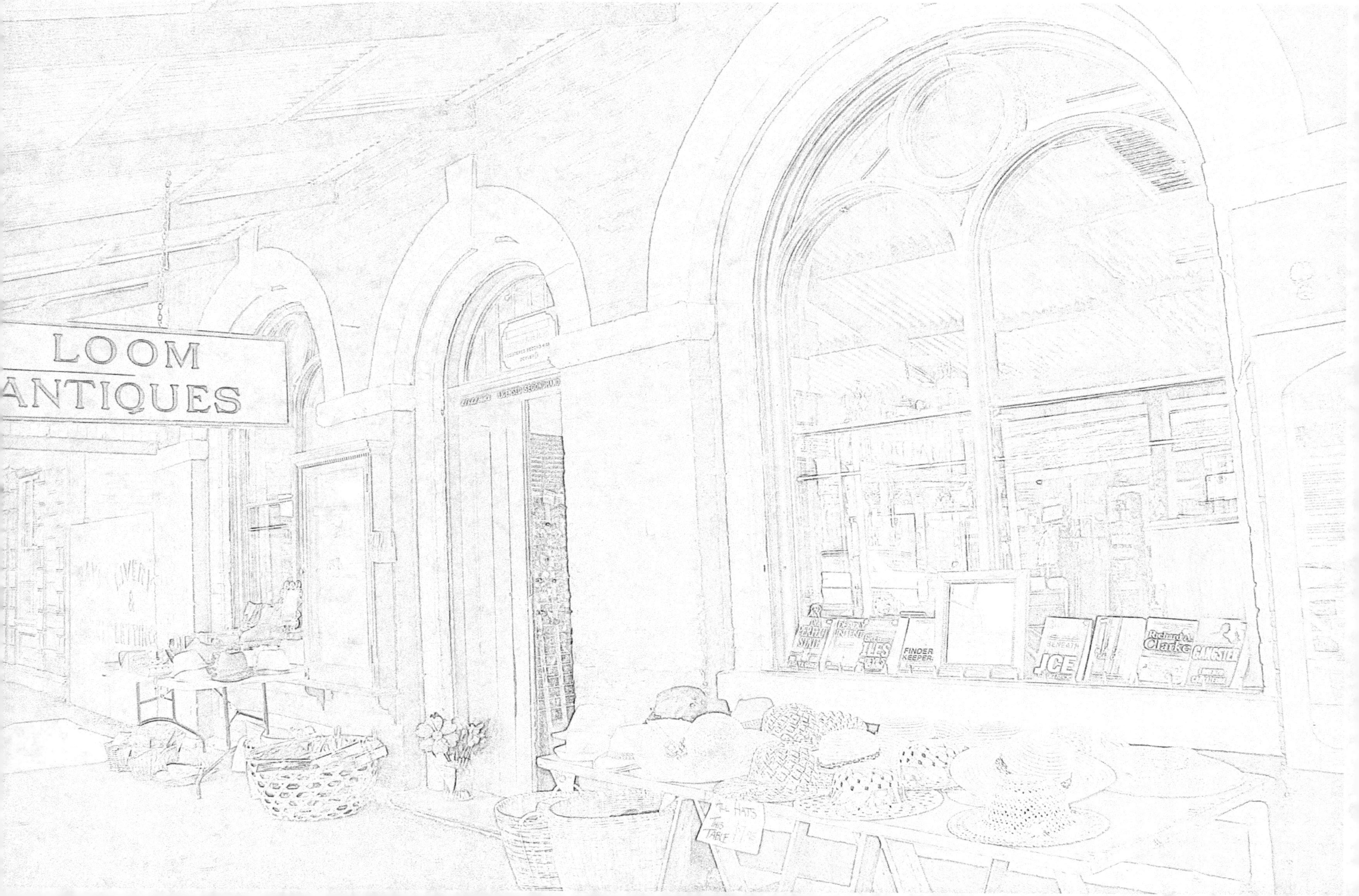

LOOM
ANTIQUES
LICENSED SECONDHAND
FINDER KEEPER
Richard A. Clarke
ICE
ALL HATS

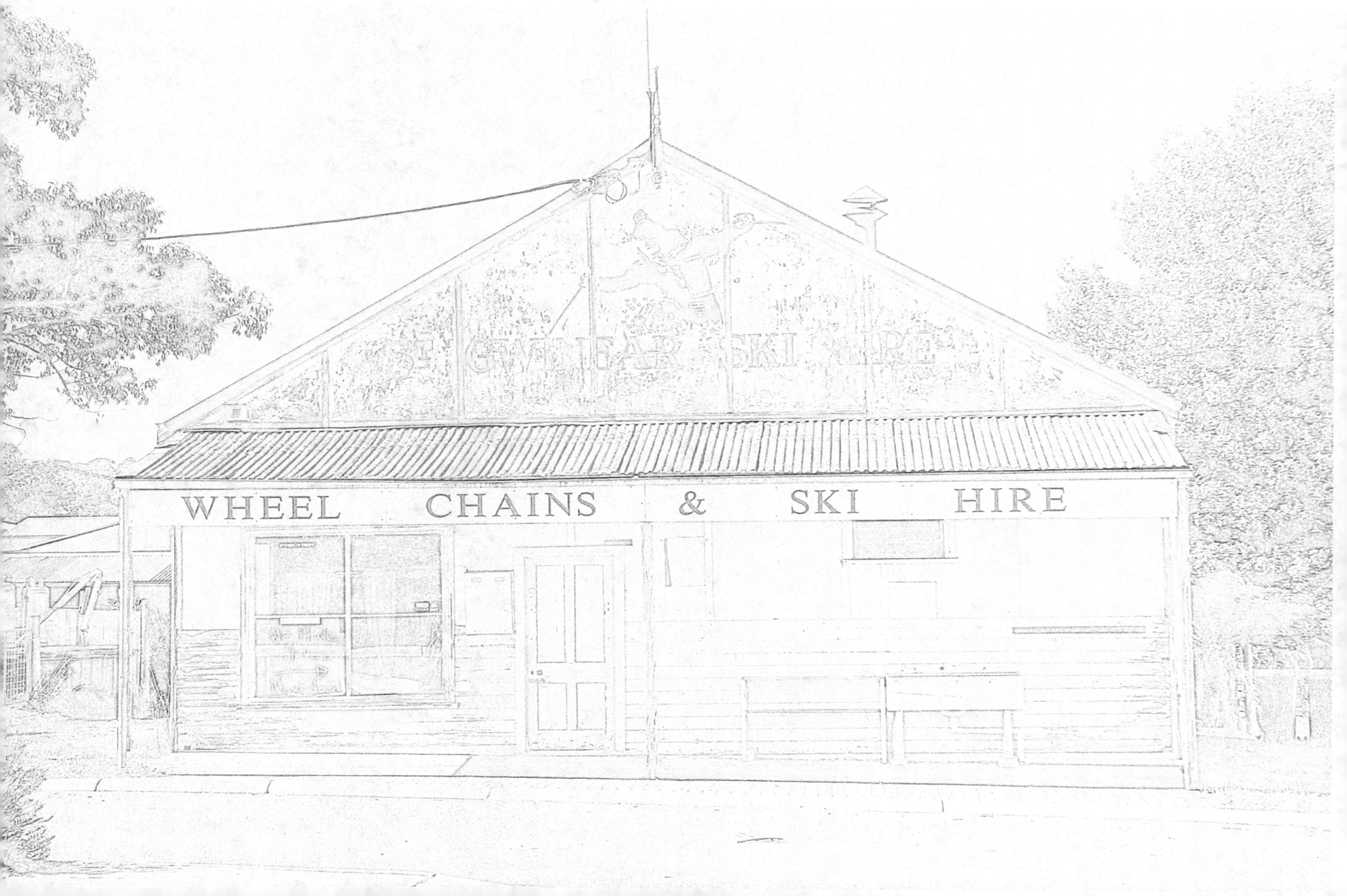
WHEEL CHAINS & SKI HIRE

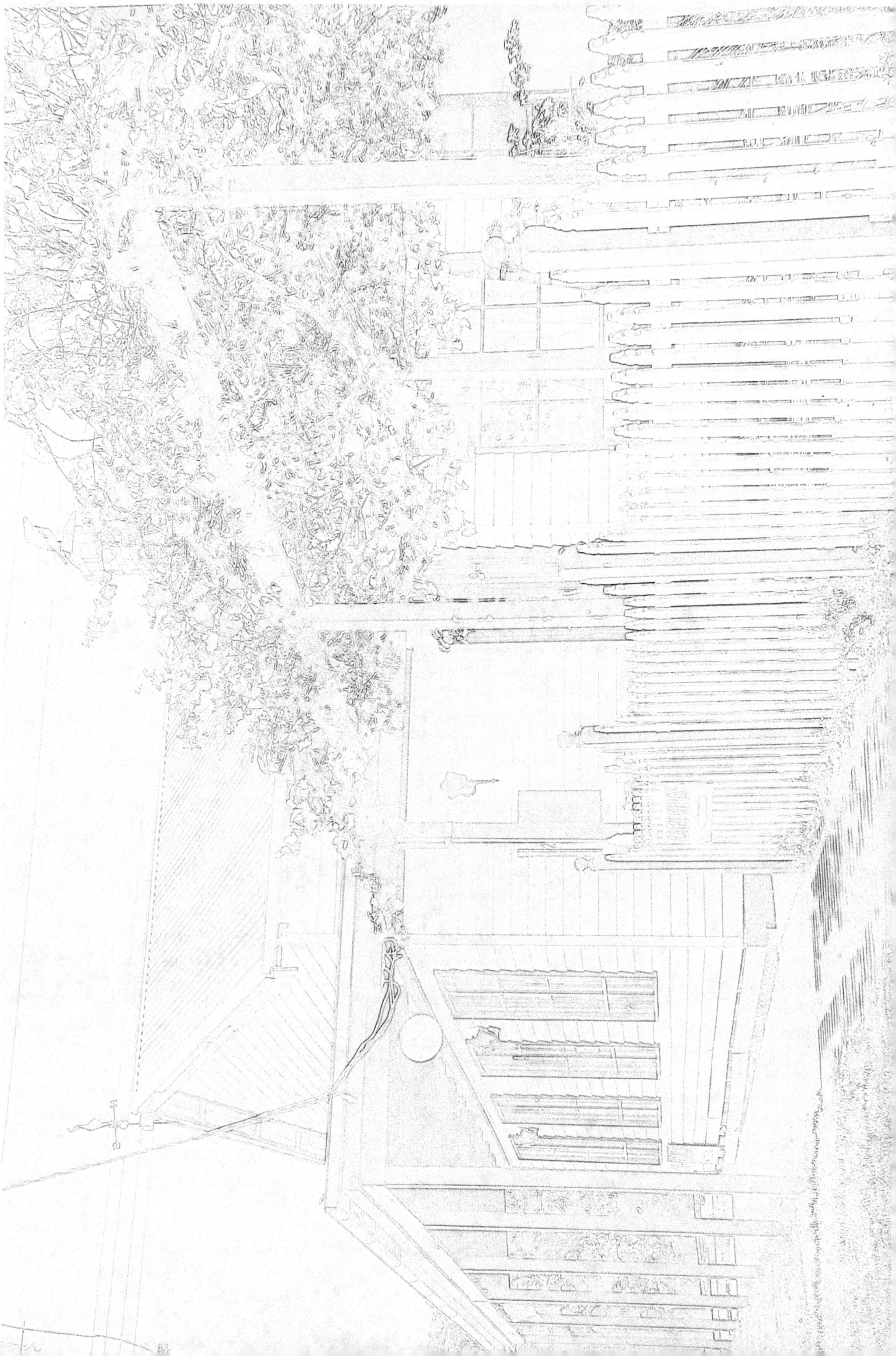

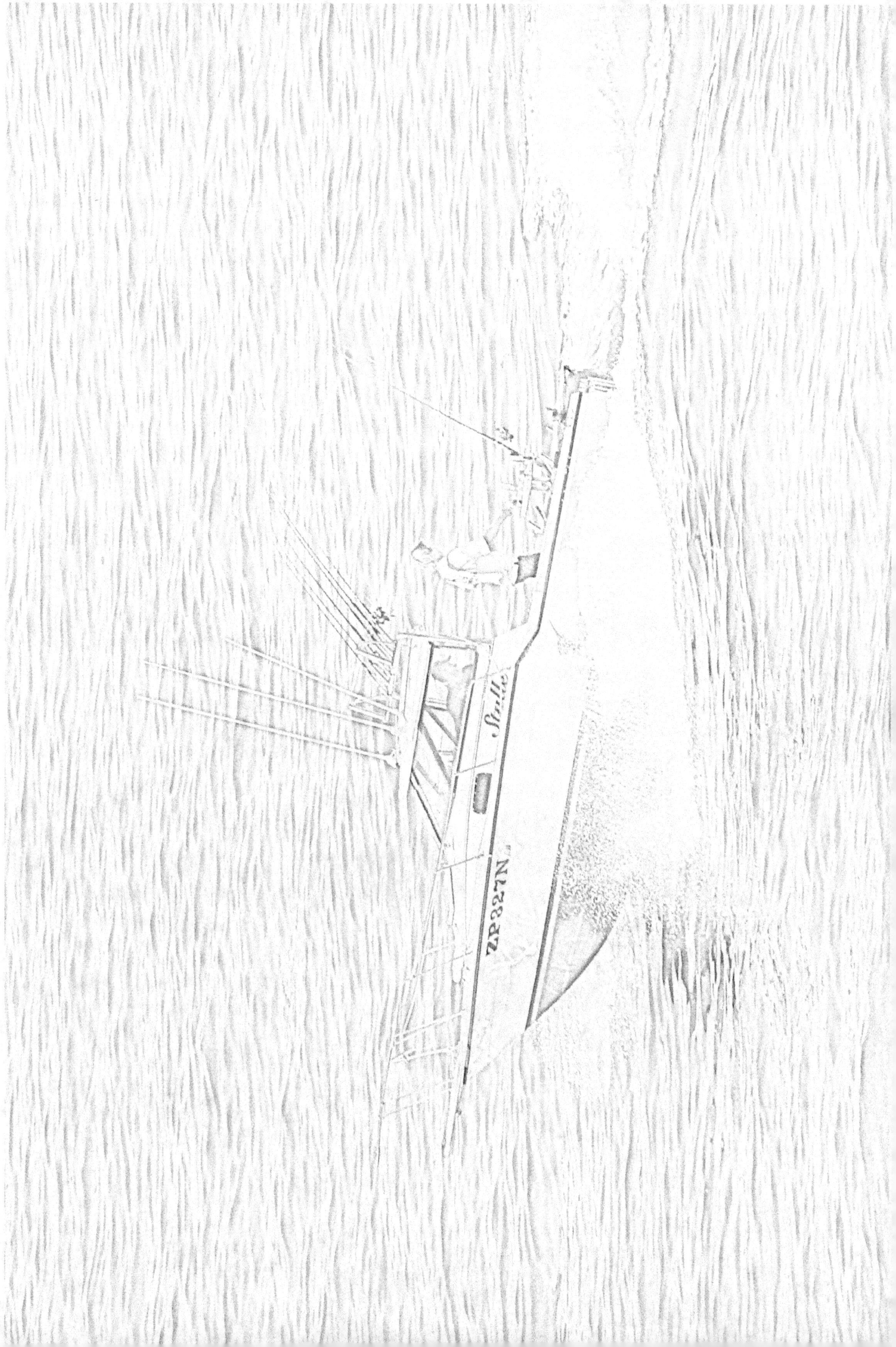
ZP327N

COURT HOUSE
MAFFRA INFORMATION CENTRE
MAFFRA SOUVENIRS AND LOCAL WINES FOR SALE
MOTOR
Visitor Information
Pino Deriu Gemstone & Mineral Collection

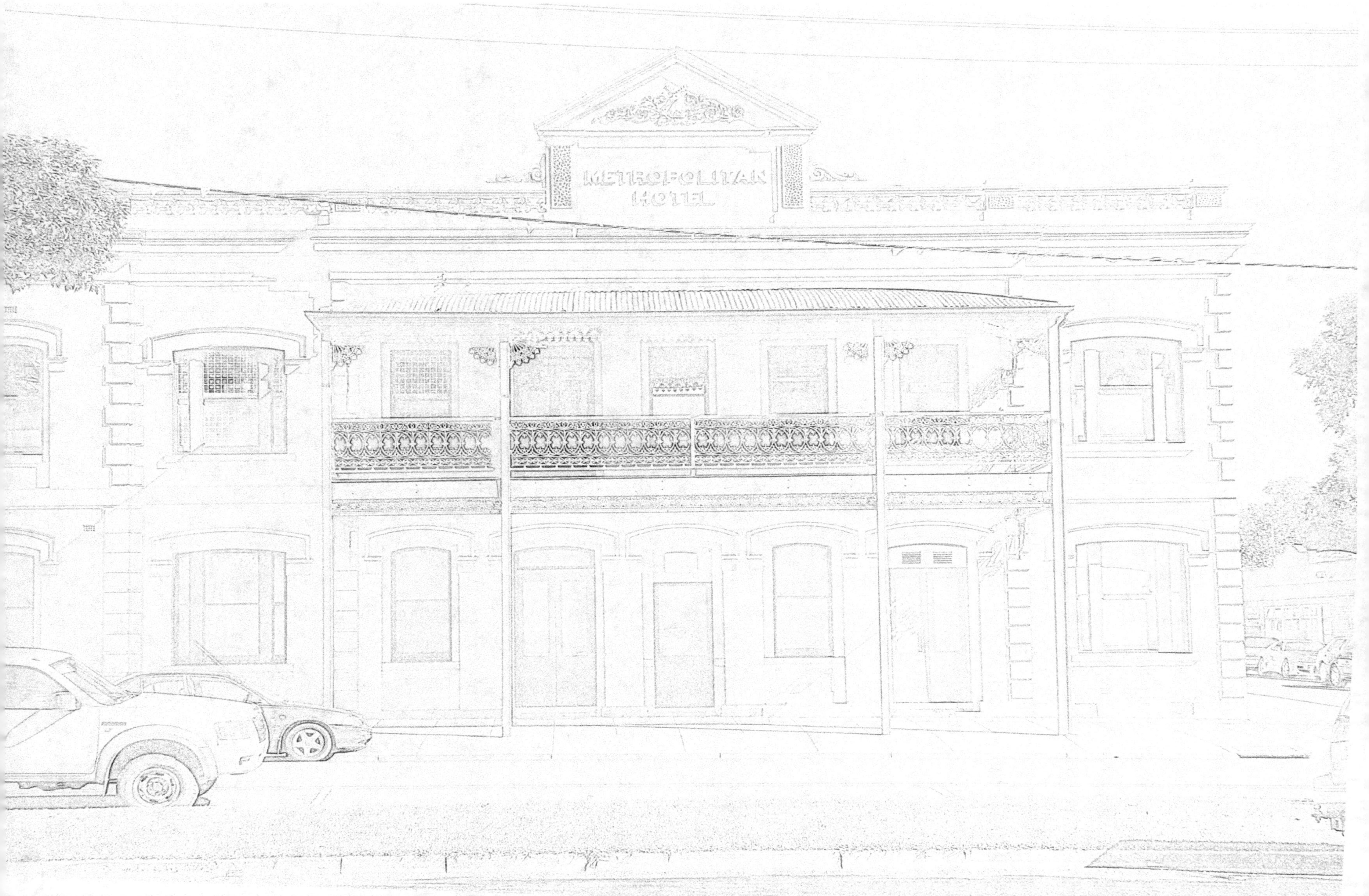
METROPOLITAN
HOTEL

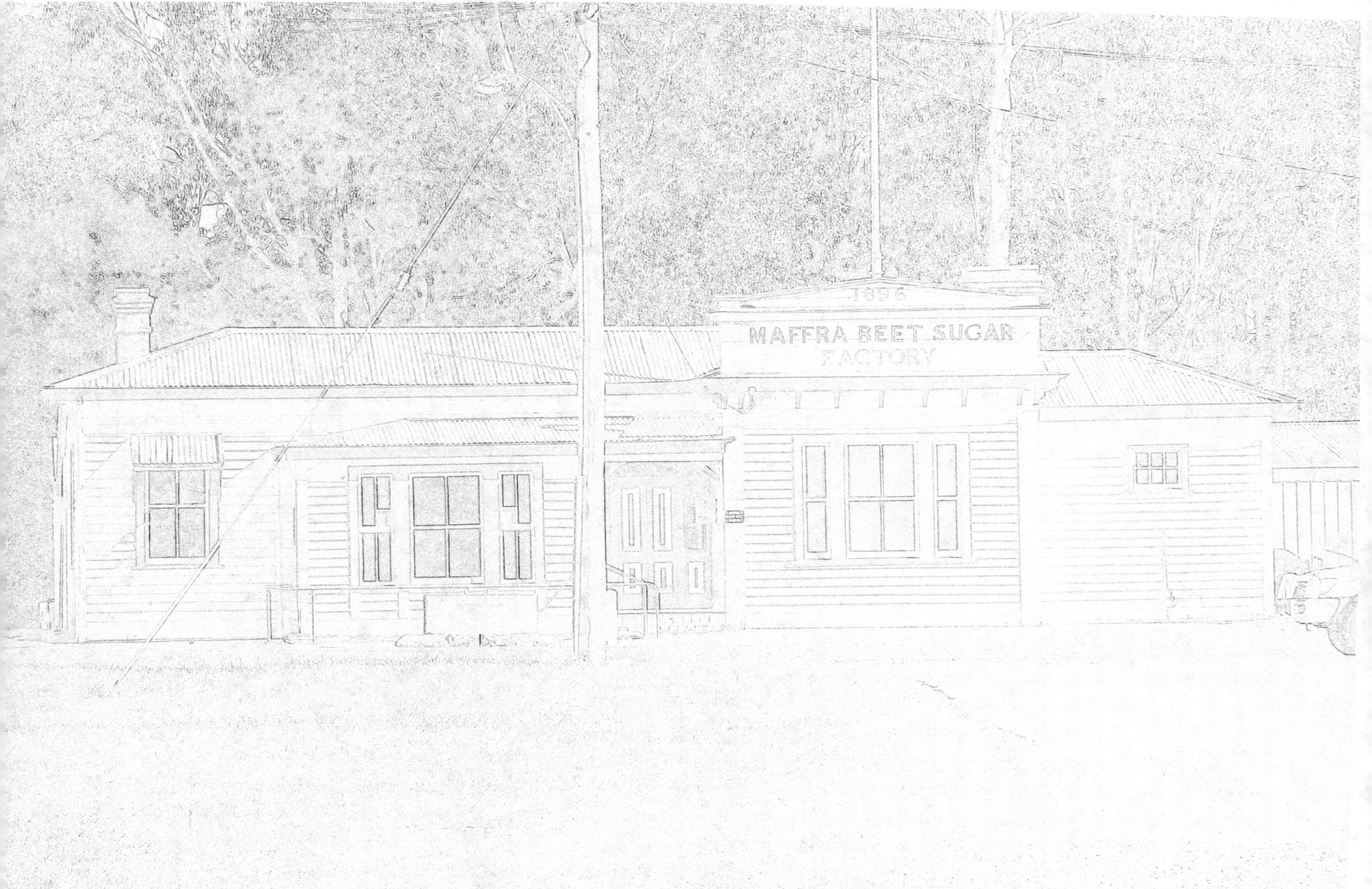
1896
MAFFRA BEET SUGAR
FACTORY

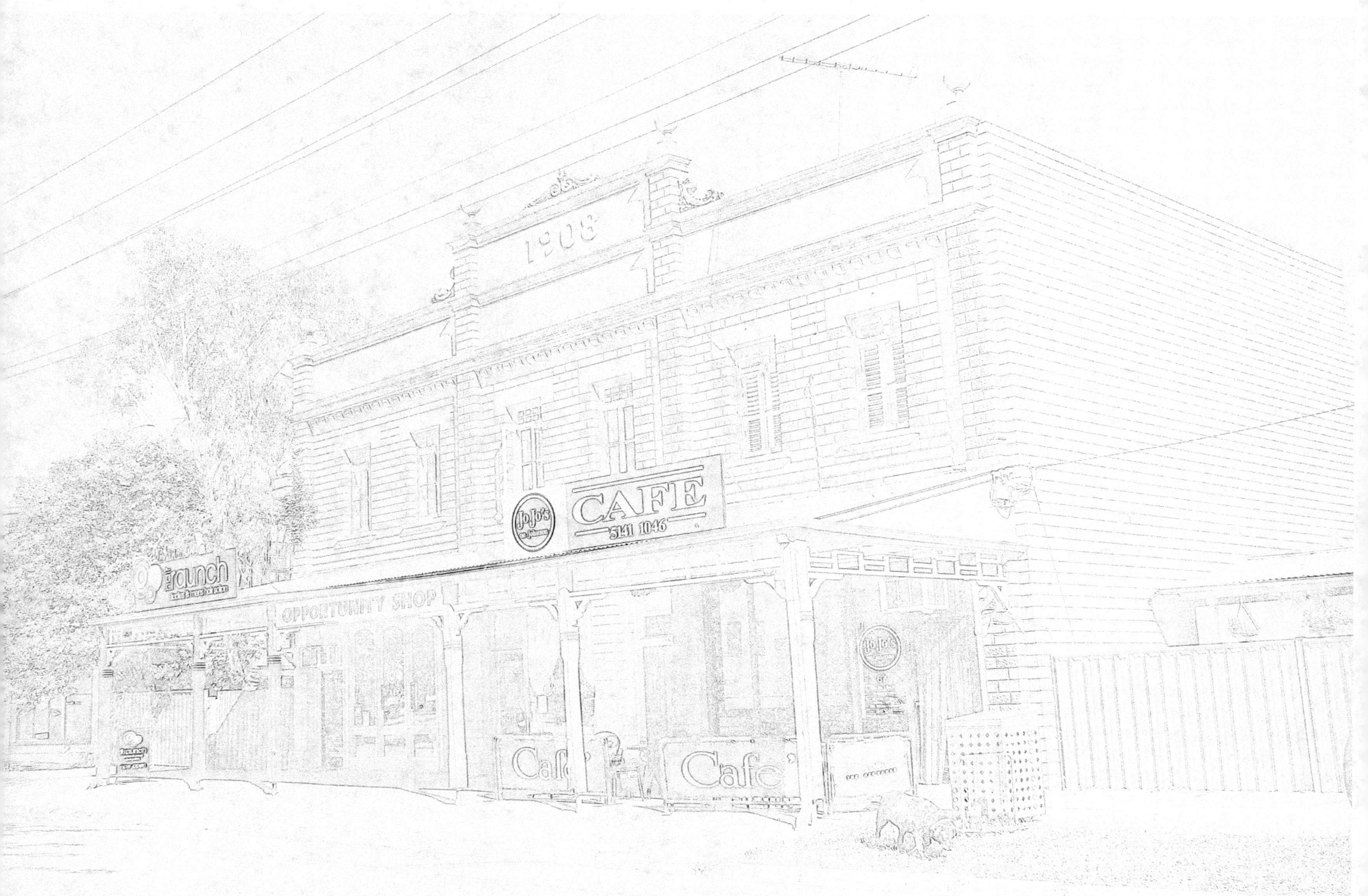
1903
CAFE
5141 1046
Jo Jo's
OPPORTUNITY SHOP
Cafe
Cafe

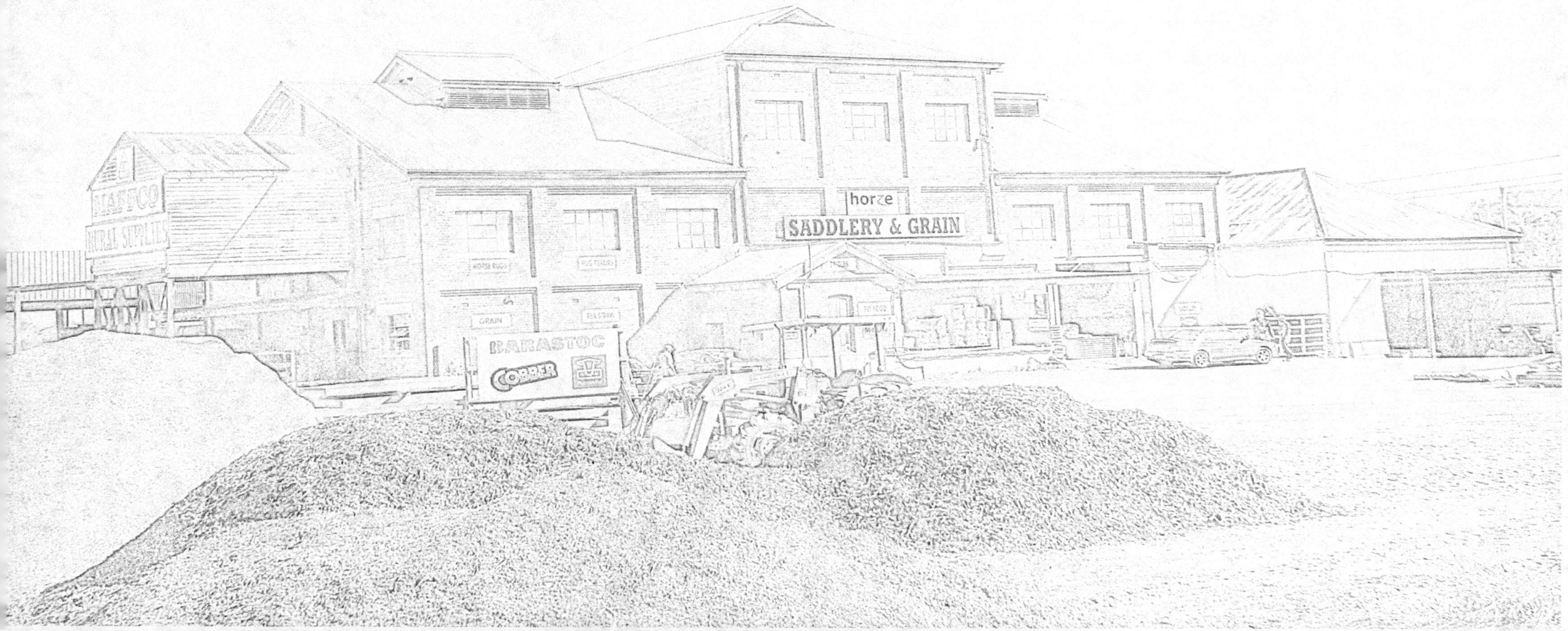
horze
SADDLERY & GRAIN
BARASTOC
COBBER
GRAIN

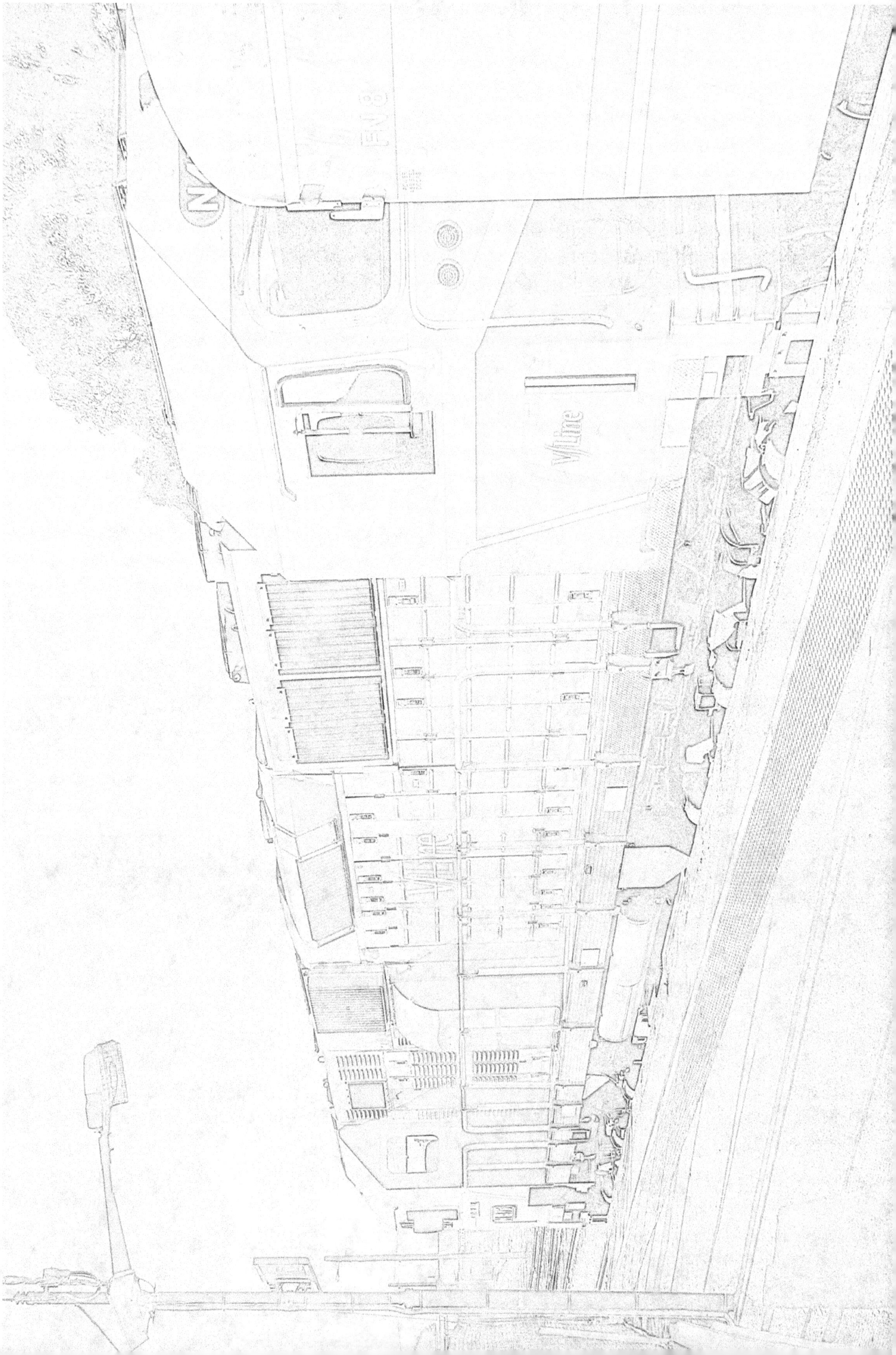

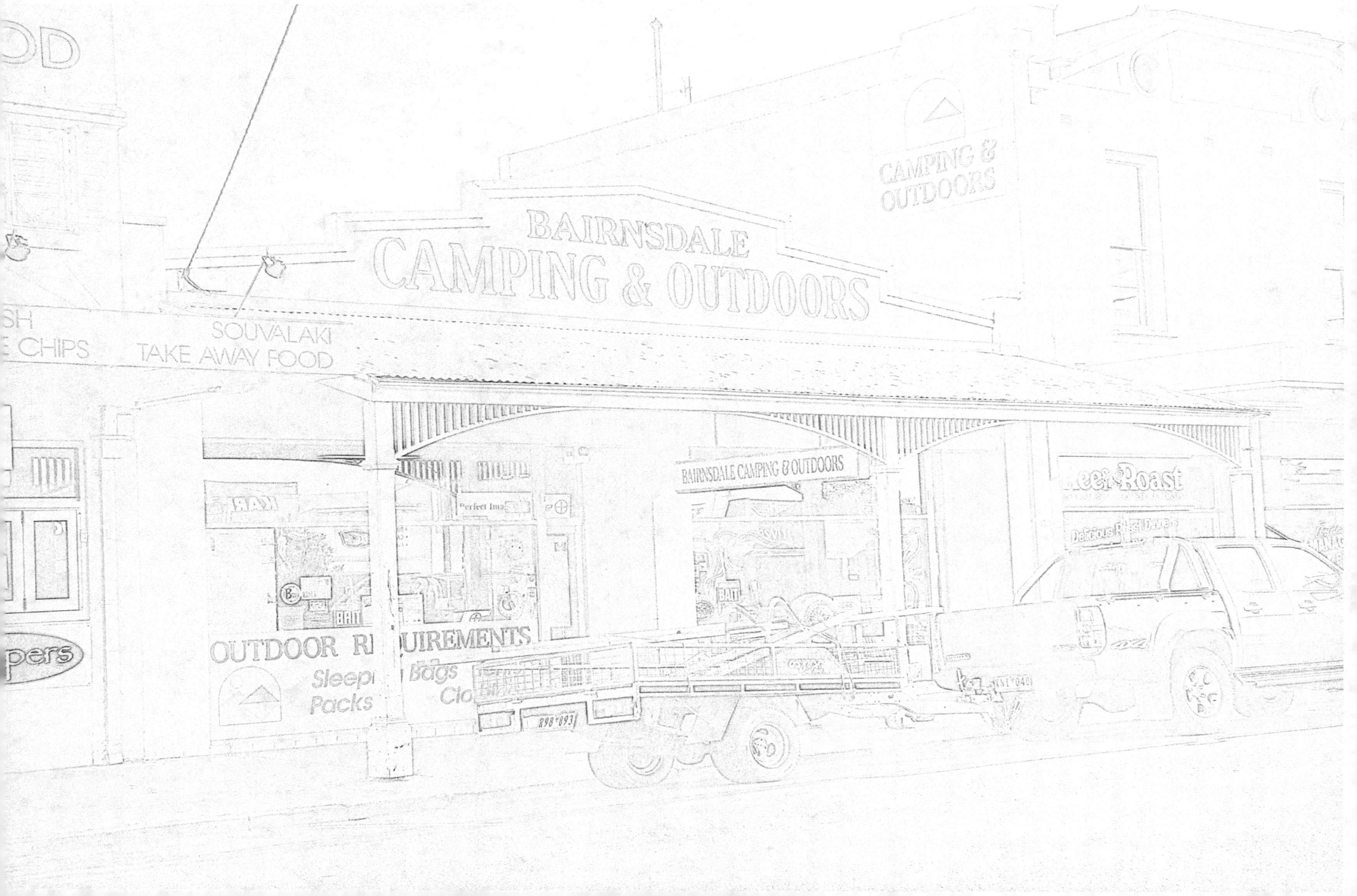

BAIRNSDALE
CAMPING & OUTDOORS
CAMPING &
OUTDOORS
SOUVALAKI
TAKE AWAY FOOD
CHIPS
BAIRNSDALE CAMPING & OUTDOORS
OUTDOOR R
UIREMENTS
Sleep
Packs
Bags
Beef Roast

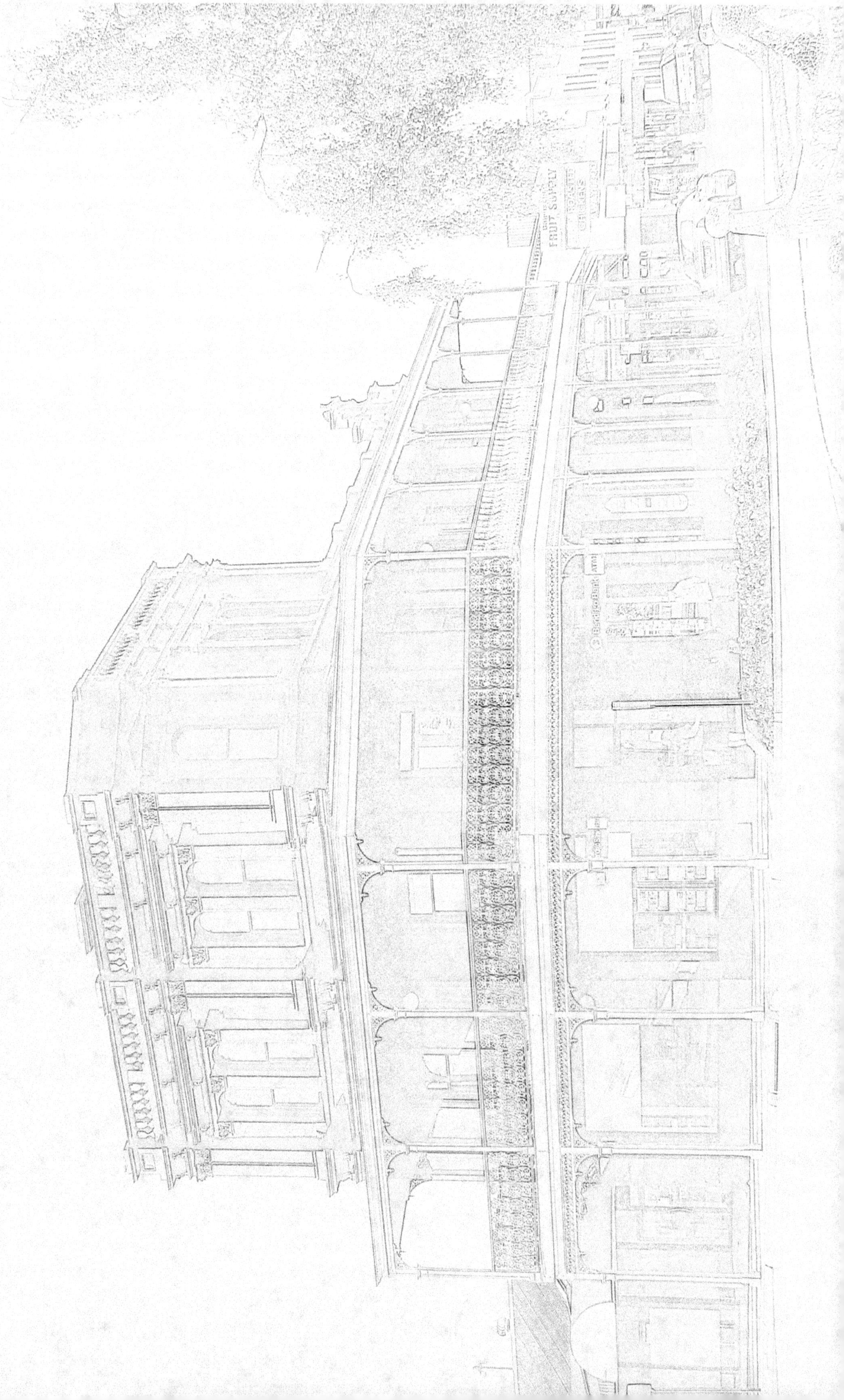
FRUIT SUPPLY
ATM

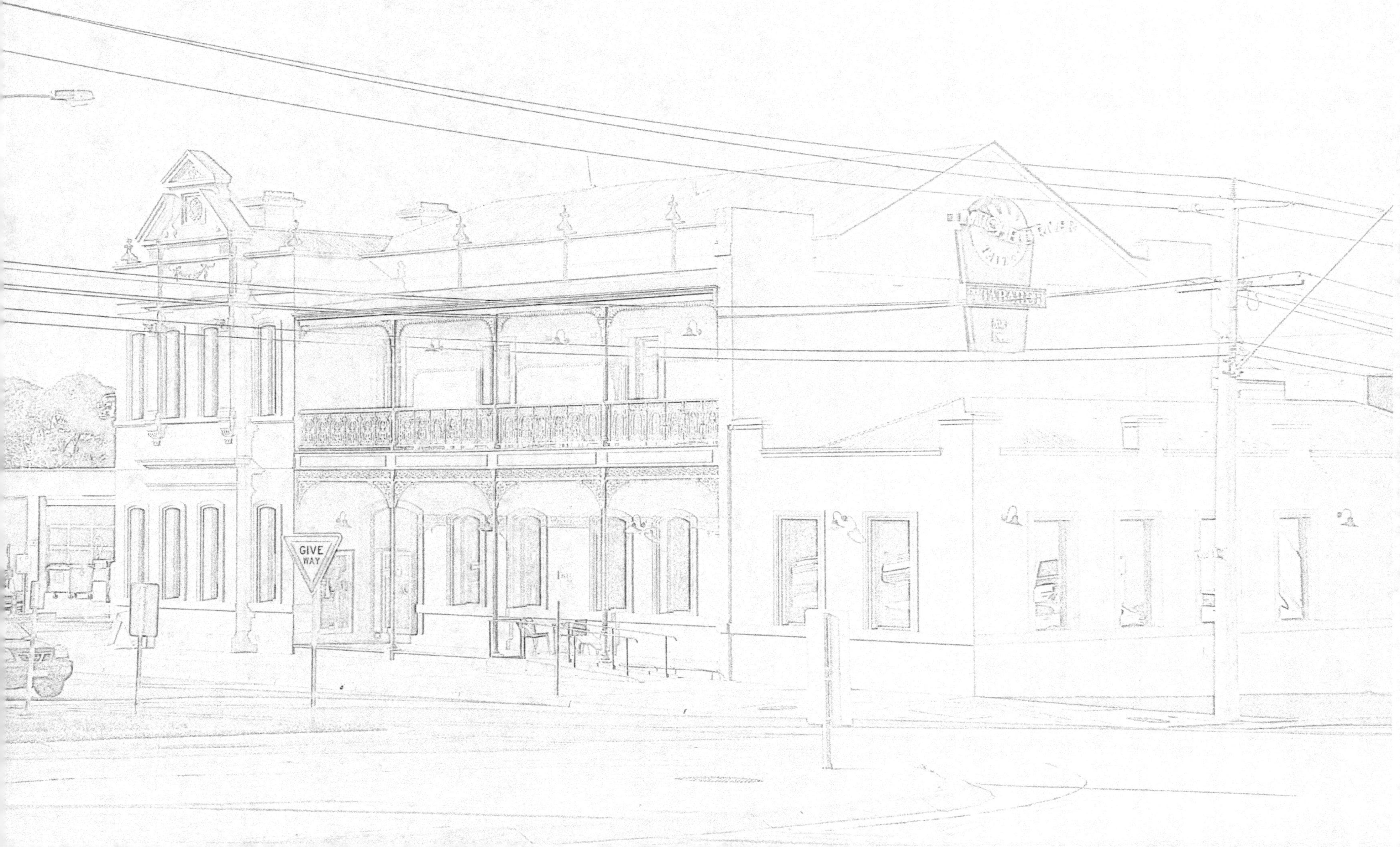
GIVE
WAY

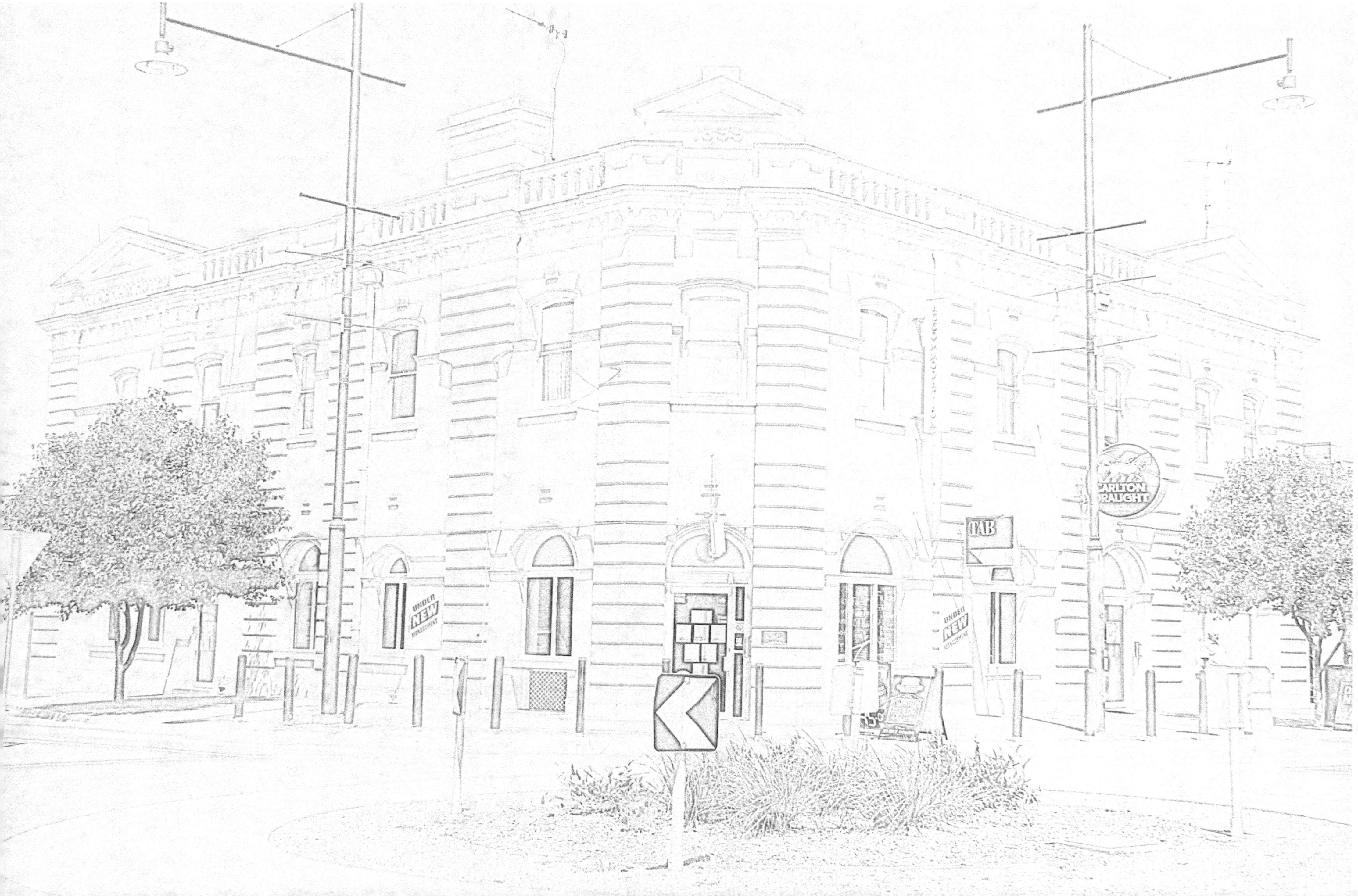

CARLTON DRAUGHT
TAB
UNDER NEW
UNDER NEW

WALKWAY

NO VACANCY

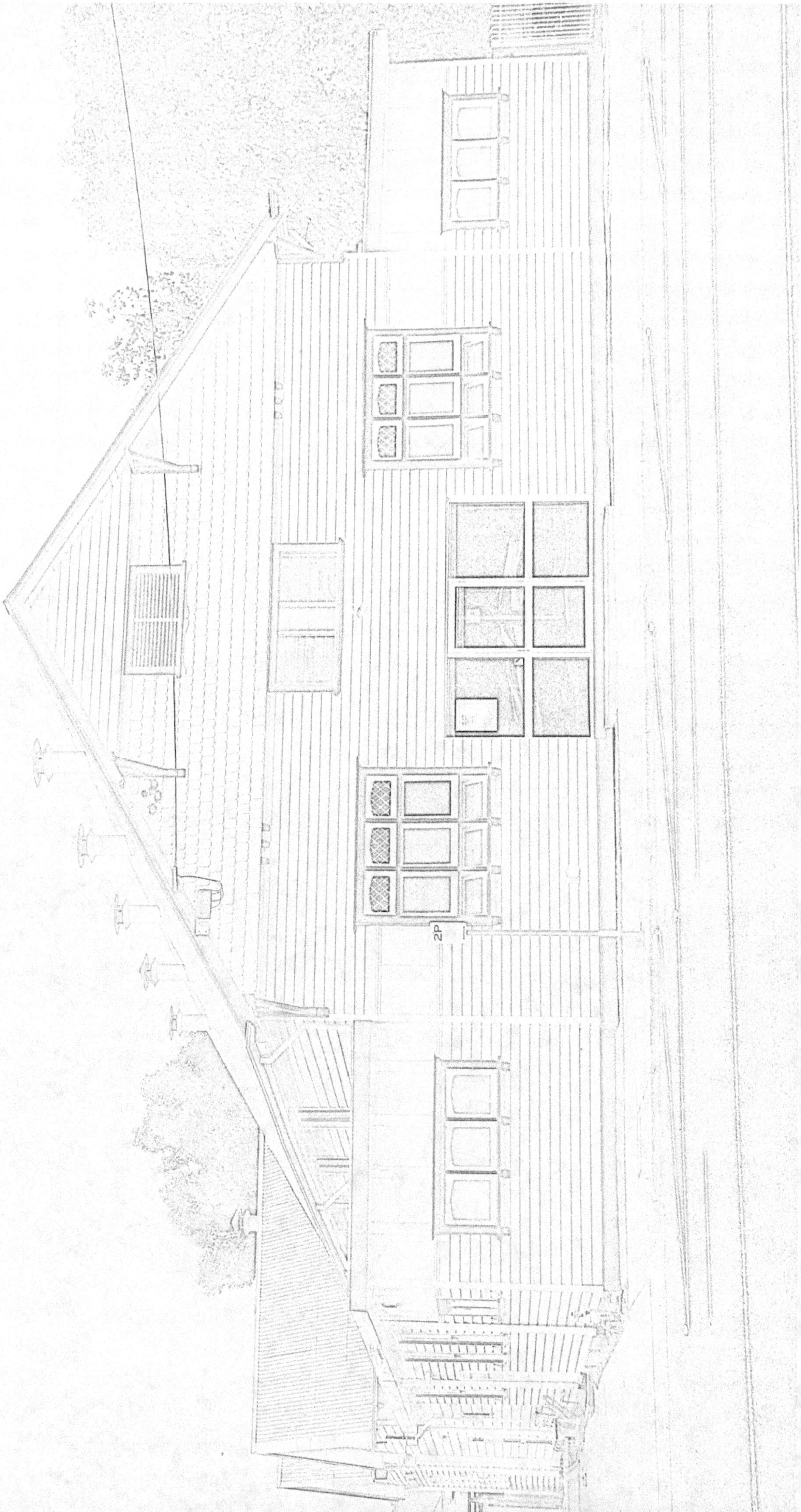
2P

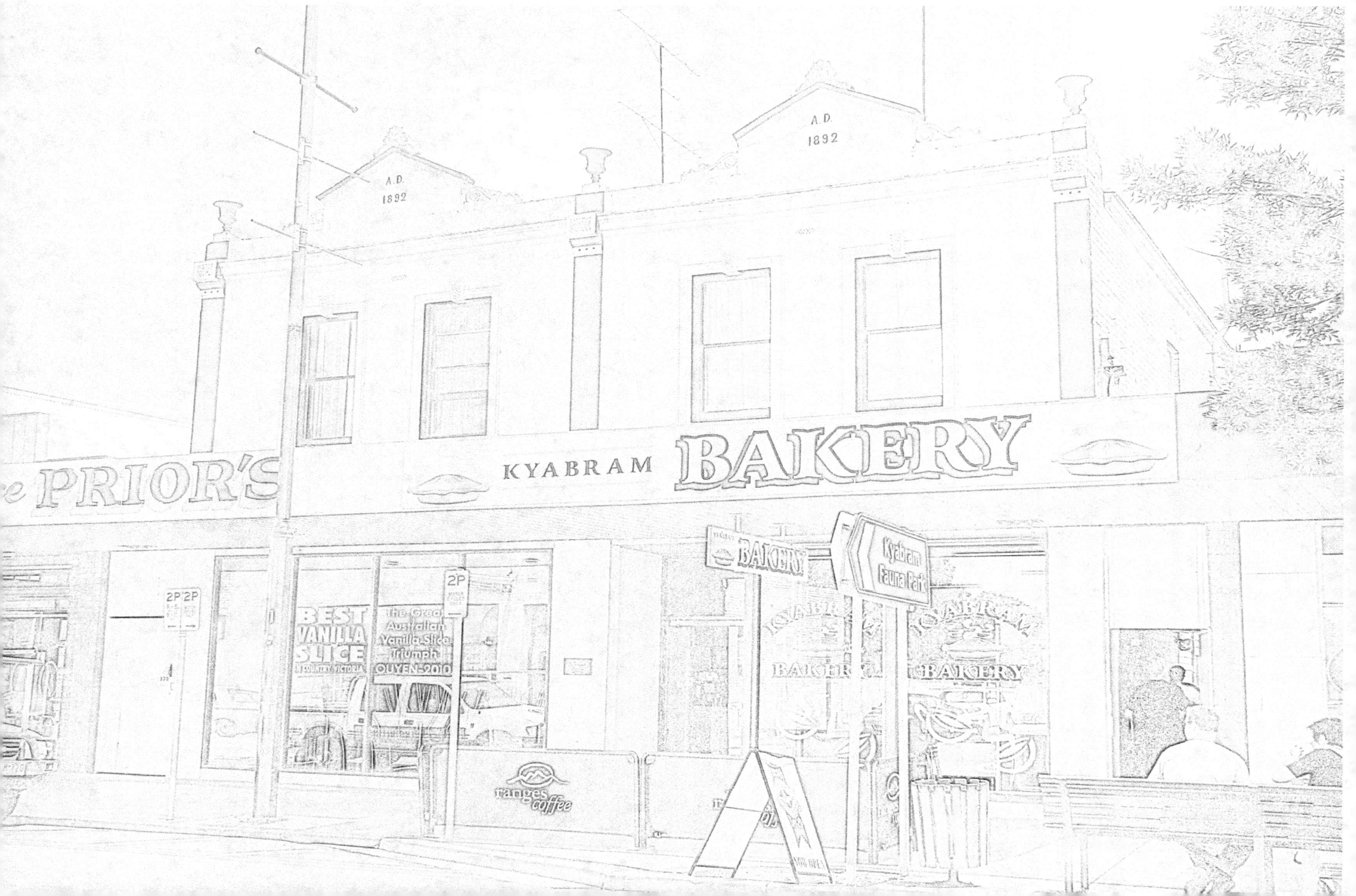
A.D.
1892
A.D.
1892
PRIOR'S
KYABRAM
BAKERY
BAKERY
Kyabram
Fauna Park
2P
2P 2P
BEST
VANILLA
SLICE
IN COUNTRY VICTORIA
the Great
Australian
Vanilla Slice
Triumph
OUYEN-2010
KYABRAM
BAKERY
KYABRAM
BAKERY
ranges
coffee

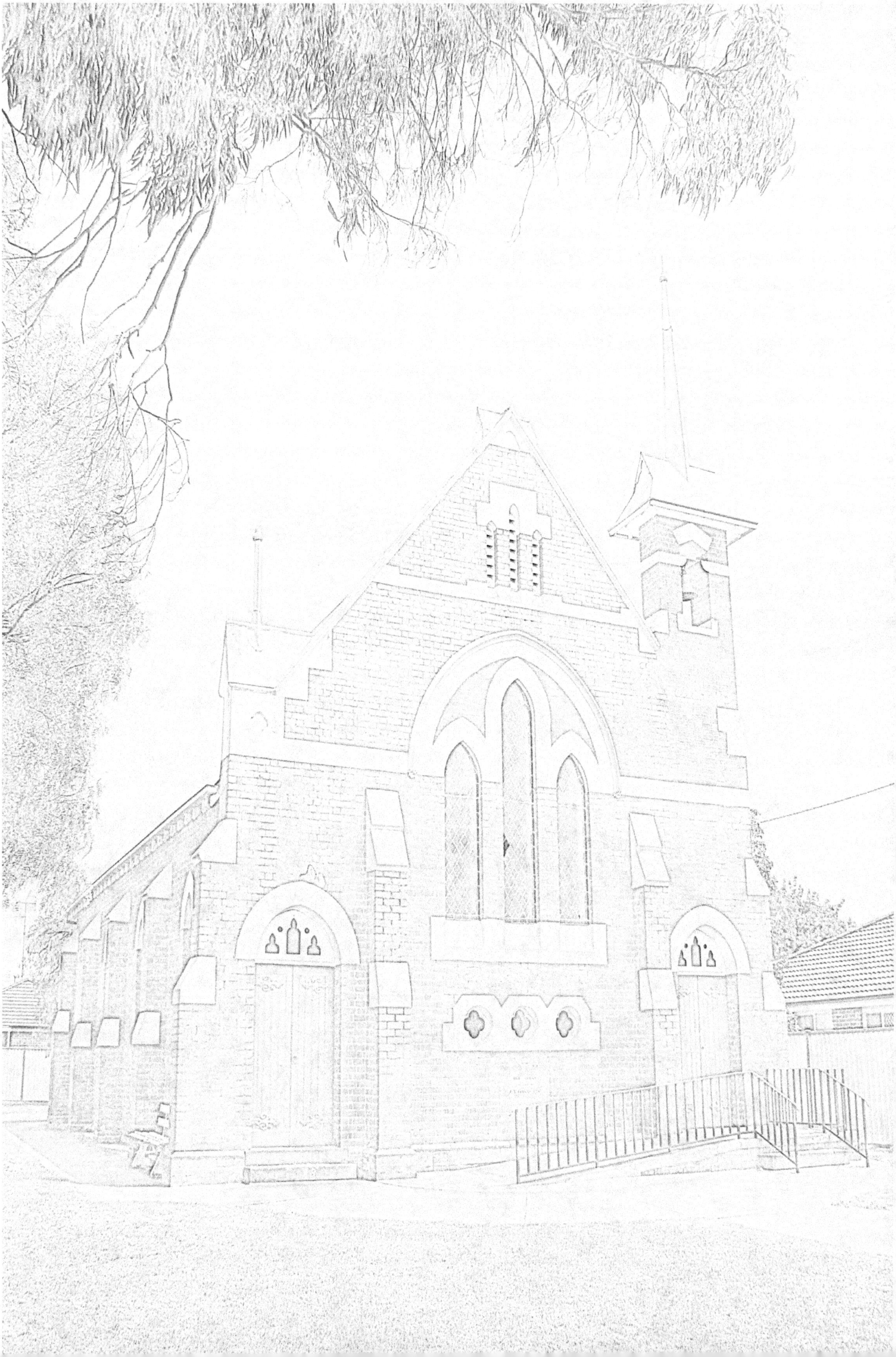

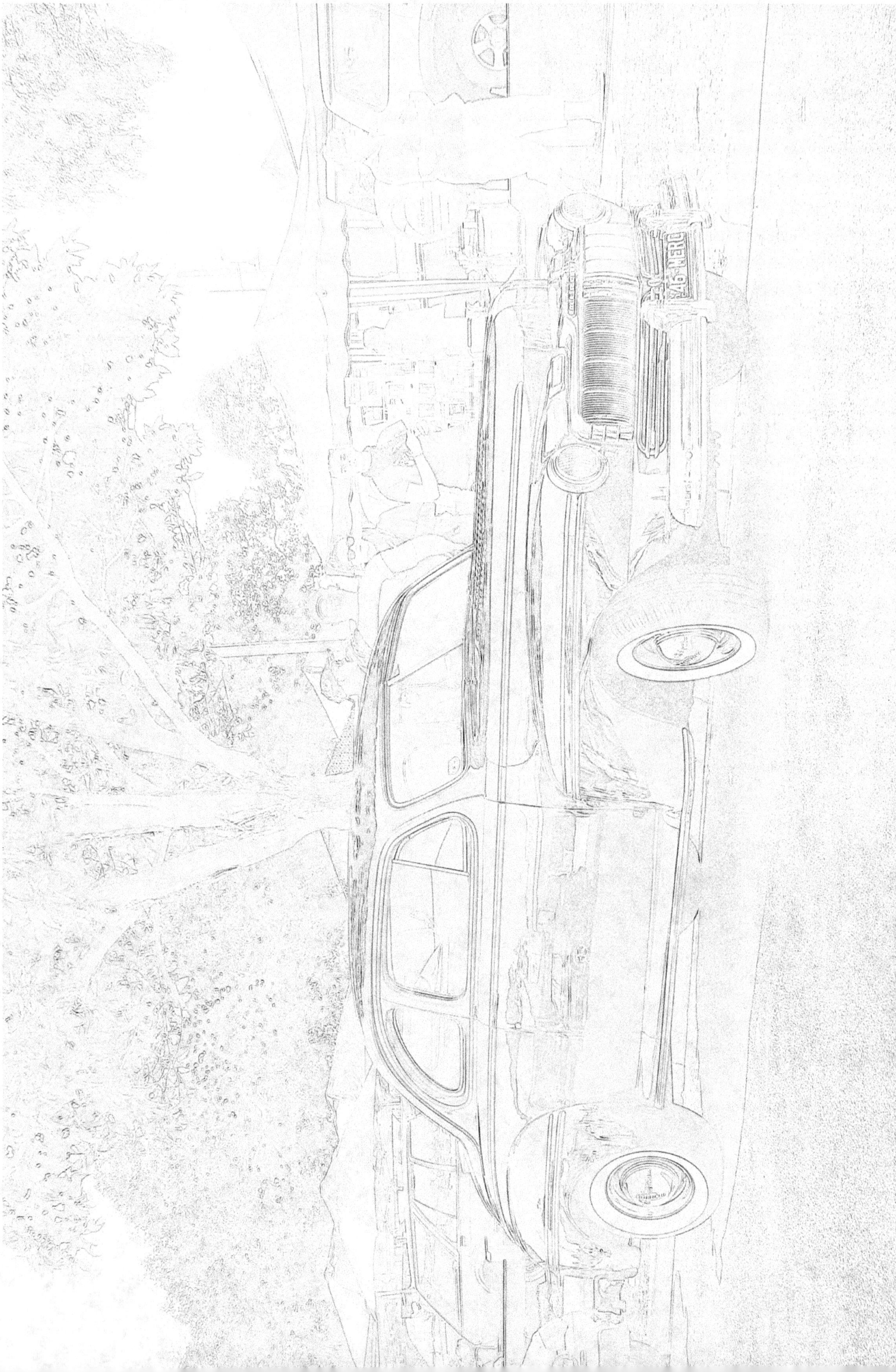

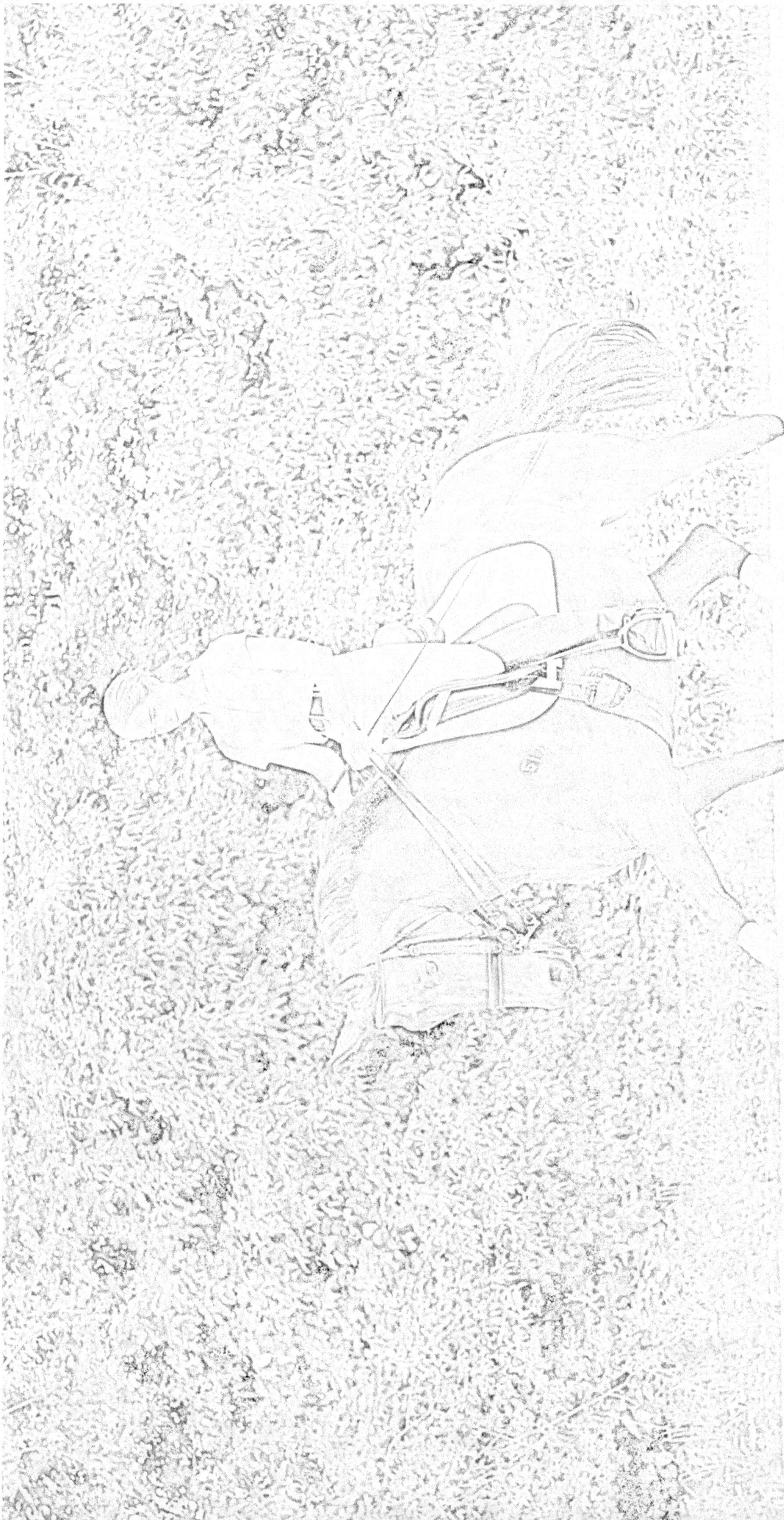

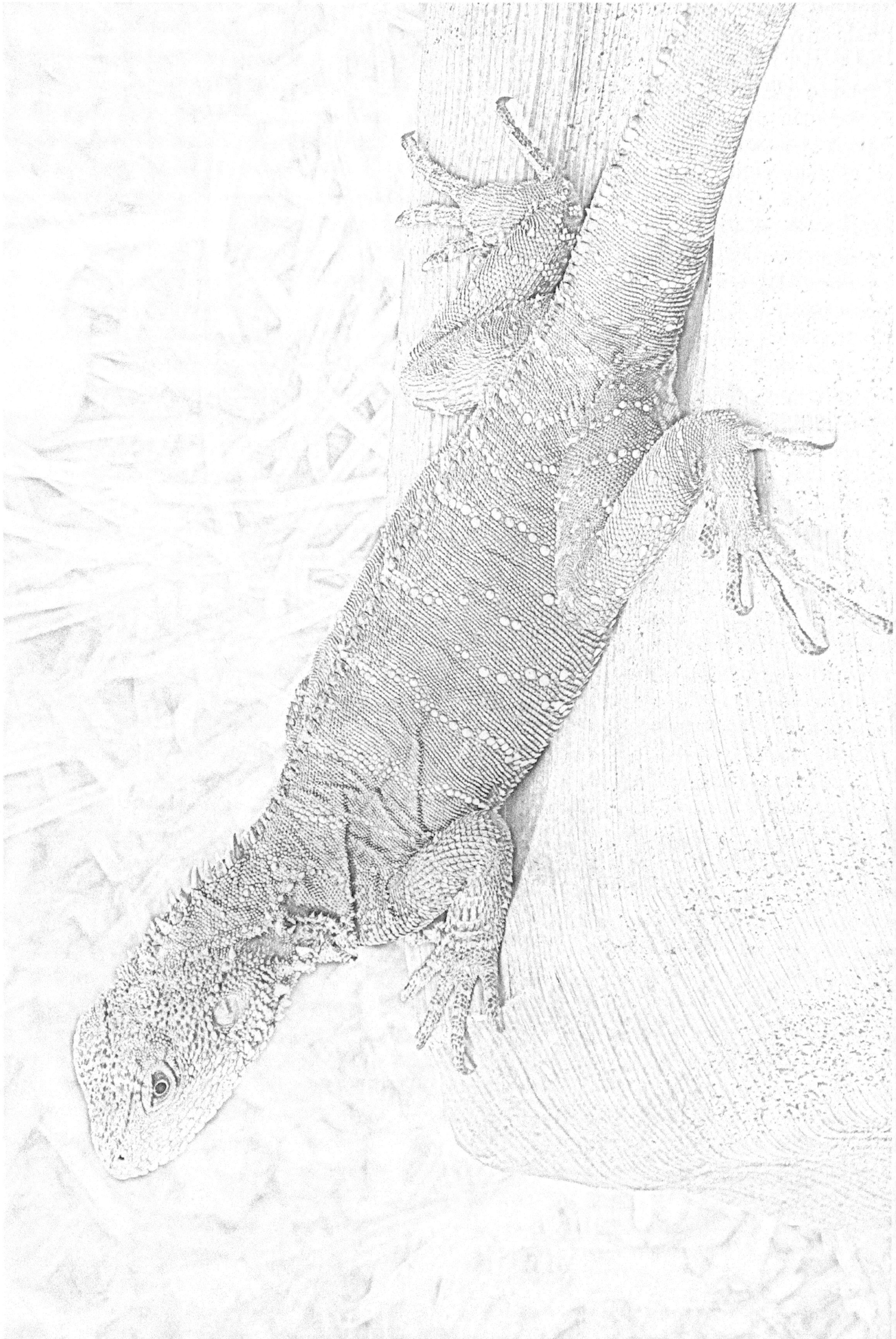

www.ingramcontent.com/pod-product-compliance
Lightning Source LLC
Chambersburg PA
CBHW081050180526
45170CB00005B/1749
* 9 7 8 0 3 5 9 8 2 2 8 3 6 *